Wheel-Thrown Ceramics

Altering

Trimming

Adding

Finishing

Don Davis

Lark Books
Asheville, North Carolina

To my parents, Hal and Jean Davis, for providing me with a childhood rich in travel and adventure, and for opening my eyes to the textures of the world

Editor: Chris Rich
Art Director: Kathleen Holmes
Editorial Assistant: Heather Smith
Production Assistant: Hannes Charen
Principal photographer: Evan Bracken (Light Reflections, Hendersonville, NC)

Library of Congress Cataloging-in-Publication Data
Davis, Don.
Wheel-thrown ceramics : altering, trimming, adding, finishing / Don Davis. — 1st ed.
p. cm.
Includes index.
ISBN 1-57990-052-6
1. Pottery craft. I. Title
TT920.D35 1998
738. 1—dc21 98-13032
CIP

10 9 8 7 6 5 4 3 2 1

First Edition

Published by Lark Books
50 College St.
Asheville, NC 28801, US

Distributed by Random House, Inc., in the United States, Canada, the United Kingdom, Europe, and Asia

Distributed in Australia by Capricorn Link (Australia) Pty Ltd., P.O. Box 6651, Baulkham Hills Business Centre, NSW 2153, Australia

Distributed in New Zealand by Tandem Press Ltd., 2 Rugby Rd., Birkenhead, Auckland, New Zealand

Printed in Hong Kong

ISBN 1-57990-052-6

Opposite page (left to right)
For captions and/or explanations, see pages 15, 36, 117, 111, 56, and 134.

Photo on page 3: **Don Davis,** ***Vase,*** 1991
Height: 16" (41 cm). Porcelain; thrown in two sections; bisque fired to cone 06; glaze trailed, sprayed with metallic colorant solutions; reduction fired to cone 9 in gas kiln. Photo by artist

Contents

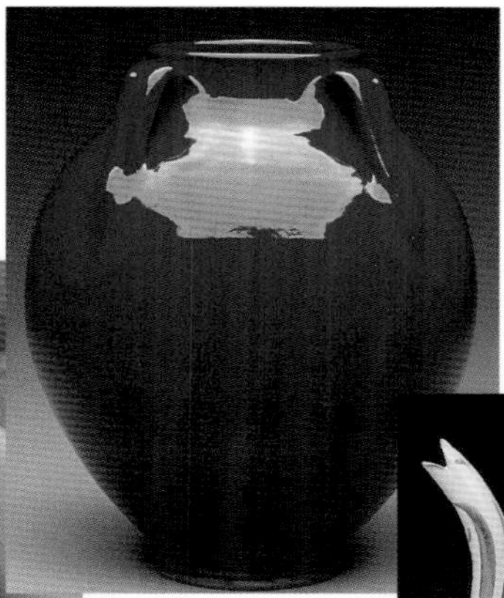

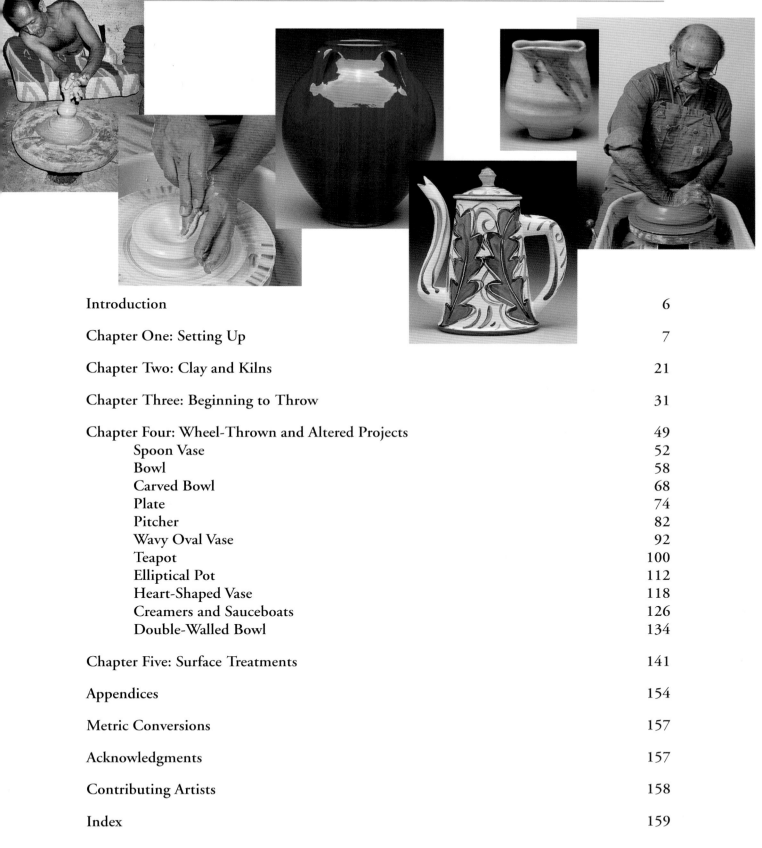

INTRODUCTION

With the advent of mass-produced factory ware and plastic vessels, wheel-thrown claywork came close to extinction in most modern cultures. Not surprisingly, however, hand-made claywork has experienced a renaissance in recent decades. In today's technological societies, perhaps more than ever, many people feel the need for a connection with the human expressions evident only in handmade objects. Studio potters around the world now produce all manner of sculptural, decorative, and functional ware, and thousands of people are enjoying the challenge of learning to throw clay on a potter's wheel.

Throwing clay is an acquired skill that is often compared with learning to play a musical instrument. I like this analogy, although learning to throw could just as easily be compared with learning other arts—drawing, t'ai chi, or cooking, for example. Like these arts, throwing can be pursued at any level of participation and still offer great benefits. Whether you throw on a part-time basis—as a therapeutic activity or just for fun—or as a full-time potter, one of the most exciting aspects of this art form is that there's always something more to be learned. Throwing can offer new discoveries for a lifetime.

Although mastering throwing takes years of practice, the beginner can make some worthwhile pieces within a few short weeks. Your first works may not match your visions, but give yourself some time. The match can happen. Remember that the thrown pieces you admire so much now were made by potters with years of experience.

Wheel-Thrown Ceramics offers the student a solid foundation in basic skills, but no book can take the place of the classroom experience. During the first stages of learning to throw, you'll need to master a variety of skills and develop new ways of coordinating your mind and body. Good teachers are invaluable in this process. Many colleges, universities, community colleges, and art centers offer ceramics classes. I also recommend attending workshops conducted by professional clay artists. Excellent, concentrated courses are also offered by a few craft schools. Sometimes, individual potters will take on a few students. Ask around. Class time isn't the only thing that counts. You'll need to put in extra practice time. Daily practice is best, but even a few hours, a few days a week, will help.

Visit museum collections and study books on ceramic history, too. The realm of wheel-thrown ceramics presents some great historical precedents from which to learn. No matter what your own personal direction is, all forms of wheel work are potentially inspiring. This book includes photos of a wide range of ceramic art: traditional and folk work, contemporary individual expressions, and work by a few (regrettably not all) of the great teachers and masters who have influenced contemporary pottery.

Clay isn't an expensive material. It's made up of the most common minerals on earth and is basically fine dirt. Although some potters can transform clay into thrown pieces of great value, as you learn to throw (and later), you can crumple up your mistakes, even after firing, without feeling that they're precious.

Throwing well requires developing your senses as well as your technical skills. After you've mastered the basic skills and are able to throw a near-perfect form, you can begin to improvise. You'll find that the process begins to flow smoothly and your work begins to be more expressive. Your goal will no longer be mastery over material, but cooperation with it. Like a musician improvising on a theme, you'll be able to vary the same basic thrown form in an infinite variety of ways, whether you're throwing original forms or working in an established traditional vein. No other material accepts and preserves our impressions quite like clay, and each person's touch is unique.

Some claywork looks if it were born rather than consciously created by an individual. Indeed, the best work seems to come through the potter rather than from the potter. The potter's individual experience, vision, and personality play a part, of course, and every potter must approach clay according to his or her own nature, but work with lasting value transcends the personal and is more than simply self expressive. The potter, the clay, and the wheel can act together to create work with spirit and feeling.

CHAPTER ONE

Setting Up

Don Davis, ***Elongated Vase,*** 1991
Height: 14" (35.5 cm). Porcelain; thrown and altered; bisque fired to cone 06; sprayed with metallic colorants, tape resist pattern, glaze trailing and brushwork; glaze fired to cone 9, light reduction. Photo by Tim Barnwell

Setting Up

A potter can throw a pot with nothing more than a wheel, a little water, and his or her hands. Although some additional tools will enhance the process, it isn't necessary to acquire every new pottery tool on the market. Potters through the ages have managed to make beautiful ware with a few simple tools. As you work, you'll develop your own collection to fit your own needs.

Tools and Materials

All potters have favorite tools to enhance the process. Some have a vast array of implements to suit their individual needs. Some keep their tool collections fairly simple, and others enjoy constantly adding new items.

Basic Tools

For the person just beginning to throw, I recommend a basic array of tools, including those shown below.

- A small synthetic sponge or natural "elephant ear" sea sponge. You'll use this to apply water to your clay as you throw it, to mop away excess water, and to smooth the clay.
- A cutoff wire. This is simply a length of wire (or twisted wires), sometimes with handles, that's used to slice slabs from a fresh block of clay and to separate a thrown piece from the wheel. Twisted wires leave a texture in the clay that helps prevent thrown forms from sticking back onto the wheel. This texture can also be used as a design element and enhanced by braiding thicker strands of wire.
- A needle tool. This large needle, set into a handle, is the tool potters use to cut and pierce soft clay.
- A wooden cutting stick. The pointed end is used to cut away excess clay from the base of a thrown piece, and the rounded end is used to smooth and compress clay after trimming. (See page 10 for a description of trimming.)
- A shaping rib with one flat edge and one curved edge. This is the tool used to shape and straighten the wall of a thrown piece.
- A potter's wheel (see pages 12-16)
- Some thin plastic. You'll use this to cover clay pieces when you have to slow down their drying process. Laundry bags are ideal for most pieces. For very large pieces, you may need trash-can liners.

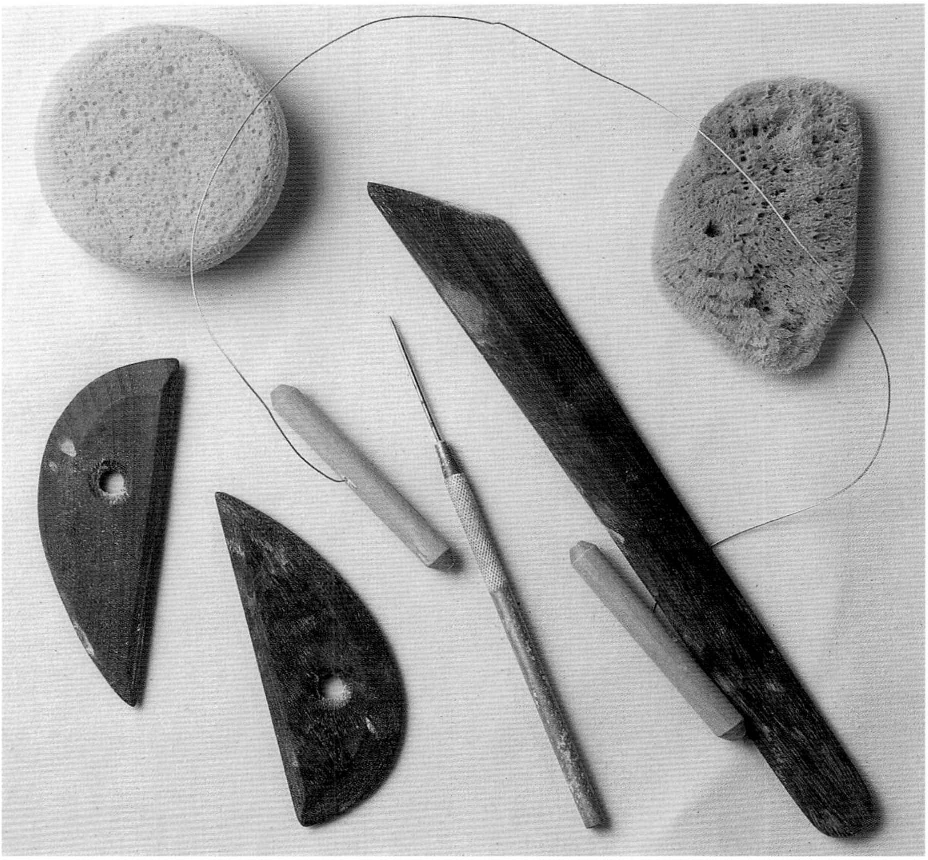

Tools for Throwing and Altering

The photo below shows some of the tools that I use for shaping, cutting, measuring, moistening, smoothing, paddling, and scoring clay.

- A wooden spatula, wooden paddle, and bamboo cutting stick. The spatula and paddle are good tools for paddling thrown pieces into altered shapes. I use the bamboo cutting stick in the same way that I use the cutting stick described in the "Basic Tools" section.
- A banding wheel (or turntable). This free-standing wheel is useful for many purposes, from turning leather-hard pieces as you work on them to "banding" a piece with underglaze by spinning the wheel while you hold a brush against the clay.
- The old sponge-tied-to-a-skewer trick is great for mopping water out of the bottom of pieces that you can't fit your hand into.
- A wall-papering tool. After cutting clay with a knife, I roll this tool over the sharp clay edges in order to round them.
- A Surform. This tool looks like a woodworking rasp, works like a cheese grater, and makes a good clay-shaping tool. Surforms are available at most hardware stores and come in several shapes and sizes.
- Calipers. These are handy for a variety of measuring tasks.
- A cheese cutter. This tool is used to facet clay forms.
- An assortment of ribs, including one with a serrated edge. These will help you shape, smooth, and texture your thrown forms.
- A piece of chamois. This works well for smoothing the rim of a thrown form.
- A scoring tool or a sharp-tined kitchen fork. Either implement works well for scratching (or scoring) clay before two pieces of clay are joined together.
- A fettling knife. The most versatile knife for a potter, this tool can be used to cut clay and to make holes in it.

■ A wire loop tool, a drill bit, and a hollow tube hole punch. The last two items make holes in clay; the first is used to carve it.

■ A spray bottle filled with water. You'll mist your clay to help keep it moist while you're working on it.

■ Pot lifters (not shown). These thin, L-shaped metal devices are used for lifting a pot from the wheel without distorting it too much. You hold one in each hand, slip its flat foot under the pot, and then lift up.

■ Ware boards (not shown). These are simply flat boards (any kind will do) and are used to transport and store your work.

Trimming Tools

Trimming is the process of finishing the bottom of a thrown form by turning it upside down on the wheel and removing the excess clay from its base. There are other ways to trim, but when you trim on the wheel, you'll need some of the tools shown below.

■ A pear-shaped loop tool. This is the basic, most versatile clay trimming tool. The other trimming tools shown may be preferred by some potters or are more appropriate for certain applications.

■ Rubber and metal shaping ribs. These are used to smooth and compress the clay after trimming. (A wooden stick is also used for this purpose.)

■ A metal spatula. I slide this kitchen tool under a thrown piece when it's reluctant to separate from a plaster bat for trimming.

■ A grabber bat, with its rubbery coating, is very handy for holding bowls and plates as you trim them on the wheel. The other gripping device shown—a Giffin Grip—is good for holding thrown forms with a higher center of gravity and will also automatically center them for you. Although these trimming holders are convenient, they're not essential. A piece to be trimmed can be tapped to the center of an ordinary bat and held down with wads of moist clay, instead. Some potters make trimming surfaces by gluing thin pieces of foam rubber onto bats. I've had good service from a bat over which I stretched a padded toilet-seat cover.

Tools for Glazing

The photo on the opposite page shows some of the tools I use for glazing. (See chapter 5 for descriptions of surface-treatment processes.)

■ Pullover pants and a shop apron. I started wearing these a few years ago to help keep clay and glaze materials from getting on my clothes. Few of the materials used in pottery making are poisonous, but they do turn into extremely fine-particled dust when they dry. The dust isn't healthy to inhale, so the more you do to minimize it in your work space and home, the better.

■ Glaze tongs. These are used to hold clay pieces as you dip them into buckets of liquid glaze.

■ A hair-dye squeeze bottle. I fill this with a thick glaze solution and use it for a surface-treatment process known as glaze trailing (see page 145). The same type of bottle is also used for slip trailing.

■ An airbrush. I use this for spraying oxide solutions onto

bisqued ware before the ware is glaze fired. Other sprayers, better suited for thicker materials such as glazes and engobes, are available.

- A toothbrush. I sometimes use this as a spattering tool for applying glazes or oxides.

- Natural bristle brushes. One brush will do to start, but you may want to have a variety on hand for applying oxides, glazes, underglazes, stains, and engobes. Sponges come in handy for glazing, too.

- A triple-beam gram scale, a 60-mesh sieve, 1-pint (.5 l) freezer containers, 1-gallon (3.8 l) plastic buckets with lids, 5-gallon (19 l) plastic buckets with lids, a ladle, a rubber spatula, and a good respirator rated to handle fine particles. You'll need all these items if you're going to mix your own glazes, oxide solutions, and engobes. An electric drill with a mixer attachment and an exhaust fan will also be helpful.

- A small 1-gallon bucket. This will hold the water you need for wetting your hands and the clay when you're throwing. You'll also need a bucket of water for sponging away glaze drips or cleaning glaze from the bottom of a piece.

- Towels. I keep one next to my wheel for drying off my hands after rinsing them in my throwing water. I also keep a towel in the glazing area and one next to the sink.

- You'll need a large scoop and a small scoop or spoon; and a kitchen brush with plastic bristles and a handle.

Your Hands

Of all the tools required for throwing clay, your hands are without a doubt the most important. Their individual structure and the quality of their touch will shape the work you produce more profoundly than any other tool. And even more than your other tools, your hands are extensions of your body, mind, and spirit. Take good care of them.

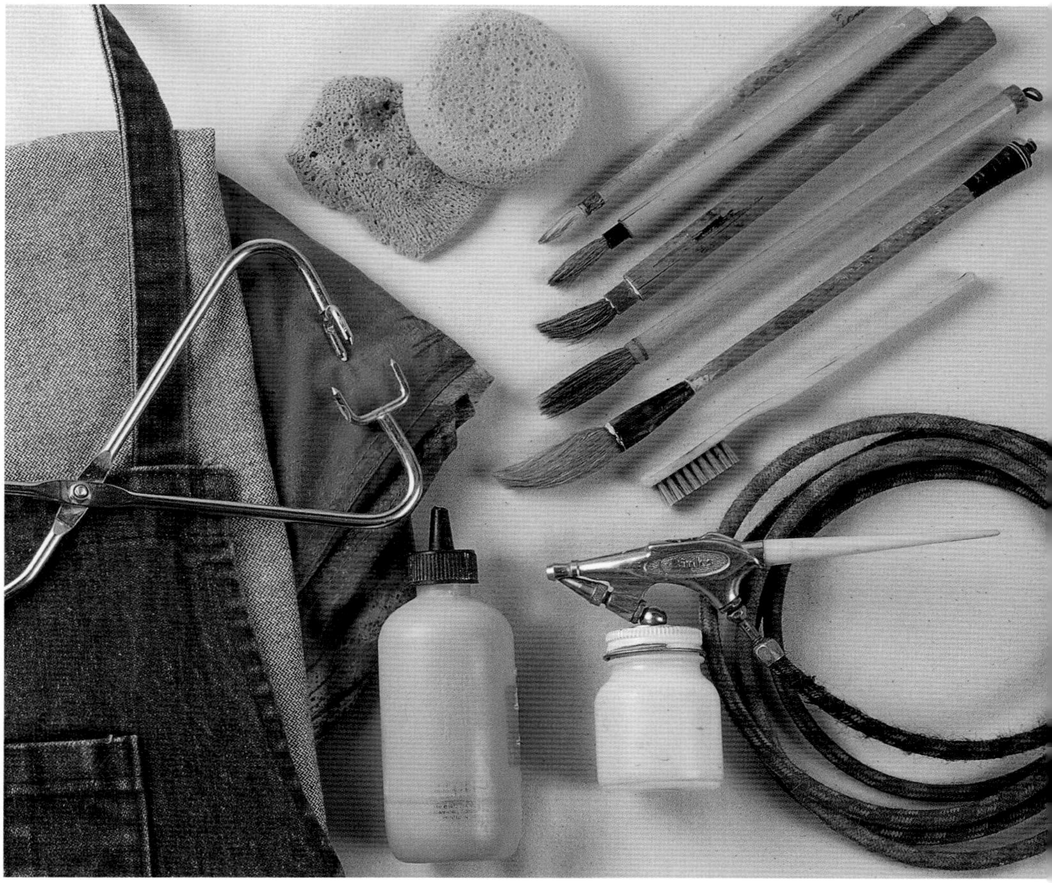

Claywork can be rough on hands. The drying effects of dipping your hands in and out of water and of having moist clay dry on them can aggravate skin problems. I apply a lot of high-quality lotion to my hands immediately after washing them, during the day when I'm not working with clay, and always before I go to bed. Wearing gloves when you're outdoors in cold weather helps a lot, too. I don't recommend putting an oily coating on your hands before wedging (oils can cause separation problems in the clay) or before glazing bisqued ware (lotion may prevent the glaze from adhering properly).

Those of us who are prone to repetitive motion disorders also need to take the extra precaution of doing regular, gentle stretching exercises for the arms and wrists. I learned some excellent ones while studying aikido, and they're tremendously helpful. Some form of full-body exercise and meditation will help keep you in good condition, which in turn will help you become a better potter.

Studio Equipment

The following pieces of equipment are ones you may want to add to your studio space at some point in time. They're not necessary for every potter, but some potters' work calls for them.

- An extruder. This piece of equipment is basically a hollow tube with a plunger at one end. The tube is filled with clay and the plunger is depressed, forcing the clay through a shaped opening in a die at the other end. Extruders, which are usually wall-mounted, can quickly produce a variety of shapes, some of which make great handles and lugs for thrown vessels.

- A spray booth with an exhaust fan. If you're doing any glaze spraying, you'll need a booth of some sort to serve as an exhaust system. You may either purchase a manufactured booth or build one yourself. One alternative, in good weather, is to do your spraying outdoors, but this method leaves a lot to be desired. An unanticipated breeze can easily interrupt the process. No matter where you are, always wear a respirator—one that fits well—when you're spraying.

Found and Handmade Tools

Some great tools are available from pottery-supply businesses, but many useful tools, as you've probably realized, can also be found at kitchen-supply, restaurant-supply, and hardware stores. You may very well find something in the most unexpected place that will turn out to be just what you need to suit an individual process you're working on. Finding a new and useful tool can be a joyous event. For years, I've shaped pots with plastic applicators found in an auto-parts store. These are actually made for applying the resin putty used in automobile-dent repair. Found natural objects, such as shells and rocks, can also be great tools for texturing clay.

I also recommend making some of your own tools. Wood, plastic, and metal are all good materials to work with. Several of my favorite wooden cutting sticks and metal scoring tools were made for me by friends.

Wheels

It's not difficult to imagine how the technique of forming clay shapes on a spinning potter's wheel evolved. Many ancient forming methods still in use around the world are almost, but not quite, throwing. Some traditional potters working today, for example, start a piece in a low, bowl-shaped pottery fragment that serves as a form of wheel. The fragment holds the damp beginnings of the pot in place and also rotates as coils are added and the piece is shaped. I've also witnessed another interesting traditional forming technique, one used by an African potter, Ladi Kwali, who made herself the spinning element instead of spinning the pot. Ladi placed her paddled and coiled pot on a low stool and walked quickly around it in a circle while forming and smoothing the piece to finalize its shape. In both examples, the pots were so symmetrical that they looked very much like fine wheel work.

The ancient Chinese get credit for developing the potter's wheel in the third millennium B.C. Its use spread throughout the eastern world, the Middle East, northern Africa, Europe, and the British Isles.

Japanese potter Shiho Kanzaki, using a traditional wheel.
Photo courtesy of Dick Lehman

The native peoples of the Americas never used wheels, even though sophisticated cultures developed in these areas and produced much beautiful clay work.

Many primitive wheels, including the ones in use today, are powered only by constant hand or foot contact. These wheels often rotate very slowly and even wobble a bit. Modern wheels, on the other hand, are likely to be precise motorized machines that turn quite quickly and smoothly. Although there are many variations on each kind of wheel, three types are now predominant: the kick wheel, the treadle wheel, and the electric wheel.

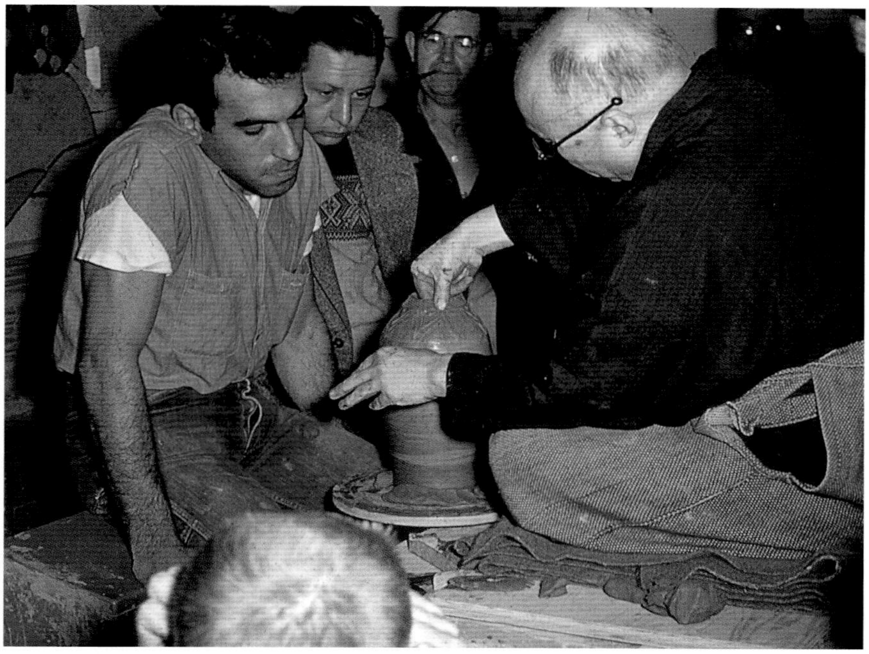

Peter Voulkos kicking the wheel for Shoji Hamada at the Archie Bray Foundation (1952). Peter Voulkos and Rudy Adio were the founding resident artists at the Bray during this historic visit from Japan's most influential potter. (Bernard Leach and Soetsu Yanagi accompanied Hamada on this tour.) Photo courtesy of the Archie Bray Foundation, Helena, MT

The modern kick wheel usually has a heavy, round flywheel, with a shaft that connects it to the wheel head, where the clay is thrown. The wheel head and shaft are most often made of metal and the flywheel of either concrete or metal. Ball-bearing attachments fasten the shaft to a frame, which in most cases includes a seat. To use a kick wheel, you sit and kick the flywheel with your right foot in order to turn the wheel in a counterclockwise direction. A motor attachment is often added for use during centering.

Woman potter from Moveros/Zamora, Spain, throwing on a "celtic" wheel. Photo by Marcia Selsor; courtesy of the Fulbright Scholar's Award program and the US-Spain Joint Committee on Educational and Cultural Exchange

Somalian potter Ibrahim compresses the clay by rubbing a wet wooden blade up on a diagonal stroke. Using only his toes, Ibrahim can move his kick wheel fairly quickly. Photo by and courtesy of Laurie Childers

A kick wheel with good ball bearings will spin freely for some time after kicking, even when you're working a mound of clay on the wheel head. The wheel slows down gradually as you work, which can establish a pleasant natural rhythm during the process.

Unlike the more familiar kick wheel, the traditional Chinese hand wheel doesn't have a separate flywheel—only a large wooden wheel head where the pot is thrown. This wheel head is rotated by hand with a stick inserted in one of several small holes toward the outside. The wheel slows down quickly and must be spun both vigorously and often by the potter who is using it.

Variations on the kick wheel are used throughout the world. The traditional Korean kick wheel is made entirely of wood, and instead of a heavy flywheel, it has a smaller, thick disk for kicking. The potter must kick constantly with both feet while throwing.

A treadle wheel is similar to a kick wheel in the configuration of the wheel head, shaft, and flywheel, but the flywheel is usually less heavy.

Some treadle wheels have seats; others are used while standing. The treadle—a straight bar attached to a pivot point on the frame and to a cog on the flywheel—must be pedaled constantly with one foot in order to keep the wheel rotating. The rhythm of your pedaling must coordinate with the rhythm of your throwing. The treadle wheel, which probably originated in England, later appeared in the United States, where traditional potters developed a variation on it.

The electric wheel is the one most widely used by contemporary potters and is the type you're most likely to encounter. This wheel—the smallest and most portable of the three types—usually has a foot pedal that controls the speed. Most electric wheels don't

The hydraulic lift on Don Craig's custom-designed electric wheel allows him to adjust the height of the wheel as he works (Lincoln County, NC). Photo by Don Davis

Electric wheel with foot-pedal control. Photo courtesy of Nidec-Shimpo America Corporation

Kick wheel with bench, designed by Will Ruggles and Douglass Rankin (Bakersville, NC). This Japanese adaptation of a Korean kick wheel has four oak struts that connect the mahogany head and fly wheel. The wheel turns on a stationary steel shaft that is secured to the floor. The slow action of this lightweight wheel encourages a touch that results in a gentle, soft clay look.

This Leach-style treadle wheel, made by Douglas H. Gates (Saluda, NC), is an adaptation of Bernard Leach's classic design, which was adapted from traditional European and English wheel designs. Cherry frame, hardrock maple flywheel, and birdseye maple and copper splash pan. Photo courtesy of Doug Gates

have an attached seat, so you must pull up a stool when you use one. (Some potters prefer to elevate their electric wheels and throw while standing up.)

Some of the first manufactured electric wheels in the United States, which were exported from Japan, include a reverse switch because Japanese potters throw with the wheel rotating clockwise, while we in the western world throw with the wheel rotating counterclockwise. Today, wheels manufactured in the United States have reverse switches because they're often exported to eastern countries. Be sure to set the switch on your wheel for the desired direction.

A wheel can add its own personality to that of the potter and the clay, and can influence the pieces made on it. Many potters are drawn to particular types of wheels precisely because they know that certain wheels are more conducive to producing the kind of work they want to do. For these potters, the wheel is an active element in the final expression of the pieces thrown on it.

Clay can be thrown directly on the wheel head or on a bat. (Some wheels are set up to accommodate bats; others aren't.) Bats are removable disks that are used on top of the wheel head, and are made of plaster, plastic, Masonite, or Formica. Some fit into a ring on

Potter throwing on a traditional wheel in Jingdezhen, China. The flywheel and throwing surface on this wheel are one and the same. The potter spins the wheel with a stick that fits into holes in the wheel's rim. Photo courtesy of Ed McEndarfer

Jose Malla (Agosta, Spain) in his family pottery, throwing in the traditional side-saddle position. Jose has thrown as many as 1,100 pots in a day. Assistants bring the clay to the potter and take away the boards full of pots. Photo by Marcia Selsor; courtesy of the Fulbright Scholar's Award program and the US-Spain Joint Committee on Educational and Cultural Exchange

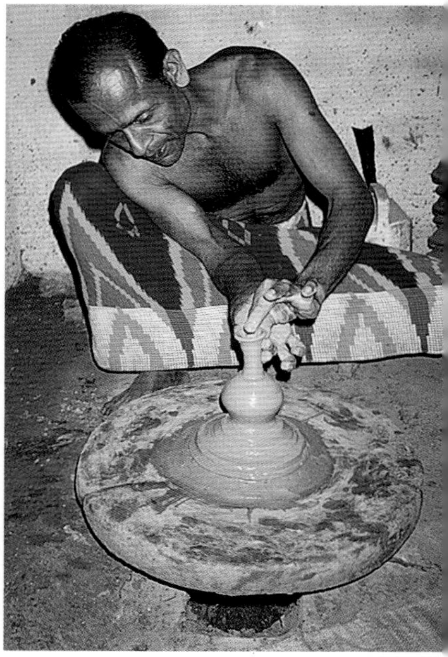

A potter in Katugastota, Sri Lanka, squats while throwing at his very low wheel. The wheel head is attached to a rod that is encased in a greased shaft, which is buried in the ground. Photo by and courtesy of Laurie Childers

the wheel head, while others have holes in their bottoms that fit over pins on the wheel head. If your wheel doesn't have a bat system, you can adapt the wheel head to accommodate bats if you wish.

Some potters choose to throw without using bats, especially when they're throwing multiples of a form that's easy to cut off and remove from the wheel head quickly. Forms that aren't easy to cut off and remove are better thrown on a bat because the bat and thrown piece can be quickly removed from the wheel head and another bat placed on the wheel head in preparation for throwing the next piece.

A word of caution: If you use plaster bats, be careful not to dig into them with your tools and watch for any plaster chips that may get into your clay. Plaster chunks in clay will pop when fired and will cause major defects in the ware. Plaster bats do have advantages for certain forms, and I've used them for years without any problems.

When you're first learning to throw, there's no immediate need to zip out and purchase a wheel. Wheels can be fairly expensive, and it's best to get acquainted with the throwing process first by taking a class.

A Place to Work

If you want to purchase a wheel and if you have some space that's removed from your living area in which to set it up, you may find that having a wheel and space of your own makes practicing a lot more convenient. You can probably rent kiln space somewhere else for firing your pieces and add an electric kiln to your space at a later date.

Many pottery enthusiasts, even after years of experience, keep their day jobs and never feel the need to set up their own studios. They find that working in a group situation, such as a class or shared studio, is more enriching. Even if you've completed a university or art school program in clay, I'd recommend that you seek a position as a studio assistant or apprentice for a few years, or rent space in a group studio until you feel ready to set up on your own.

Unless you have a sufficiently large inheritance, setting up a fully-equipped studio is best done in gradual steps. If you plan to make a living as a potter, as you take these steps, you can learn how to market what you make. Surviving financially in today's world takes selling quite a few pots. Making a living as a potter is possible and can be a rewarding pursuit, but it isn't easy.

When you're ready to set up your own studio, it doesn't need to be terribly complex. All that a potter really needs is a room big enough to accommodate a wheel, a work table, and an adequate amount of shelving. The quantity of work you produce will determine how much space you need. Generally speaking, a studio should be able to hold at least a kiln load of work. (Some potters prefer to accumulate several loads before glazing and firing.) The size of your kiln or kilns will be a critical factor here.

Your work-space design will be an individual matter and will depend on how much equipment you want to put into the space, and whether or not you want to share it. In studios where several people work together, throwing, glazing, and firing may be going on simultaneously in different areas. Whatever arrangement you choose, I recommend keeping it as clean and as organized as possible. Doing so will make your studio a healthier and more pleasant place to spend your time. In my studio, we always use a dust-attracting compound when we sweep, and we clean tables and shelves with a damp sponge in order to keep dust out of the air as much as possible.

Running water for throwing, glazing, and cleaning is also an advantage in any clay studio, but remember to avoid dumping clay- and glaze-laden water down the sink. It will clog the pipes. Clay traps, for catching the inevitable residue that results from washing tools and buckets, can be made from plastic buckets and attached to the drain under the sink. The drainpipe from the sink enters the bucket lid, and an outlet pipe exits from the bucket's side. This allows the sediment to settle to the bottom of the bucket. Depending on how frequently you use the sink, you'll need to empty the trap every month or so. The gunk you remove can be dried by scooping it into a homemade plaster trough and letting it sit. After it's dry, it can be thrown in the garbage.

If your studio area doesn't have running water, you'll need to use buckets to carry water from another source. The clay slurry that accumulates in the buckets of throwing water can be recycled, and the residue in the cleaning buckets can be dried and thrown away.

Right: **Bennett Bean, *Double Series,*** 1997
10" x 19" x 9½" (25.5 x 48.5 x 24 cm). Earthenware; thrown and altered; tape resist, glazed; bisqued and pit fired; painted and gold-leafed interior.

Bottom left: **Keiko Fukazawa, *Waiting to Fill,*** 1996
11" x 9" x 9" (28 x 23 x 23 cm). White earthenware; stack-thrown bowl, turned bottom, round clay slab set in bowl to create water effect, bowl joined to hand-built base; textured with rock, slip-cast shapes; bisque fired to cone 08; oxidation glaze fired to cone 06; luster fired to cone 018.
Photo by Anthony Cuñha

Bottom right: **Elaine F. Alt, *Waves,*** 1997
15" x 6" (38 x 15 cm). Earthenware; upper piece thrown upside down without a base, bottom thrown as bowl, pieces joined when leather hard, waves pulled and attached; bisque fired to cone 06; underglazes applied with tape and wax resist, dots of glaze applied; glaze fired to cone 01; dots of gold luster applied to glazed dots; luster fired to cone 018.
Photo by Tommy Olof Elder

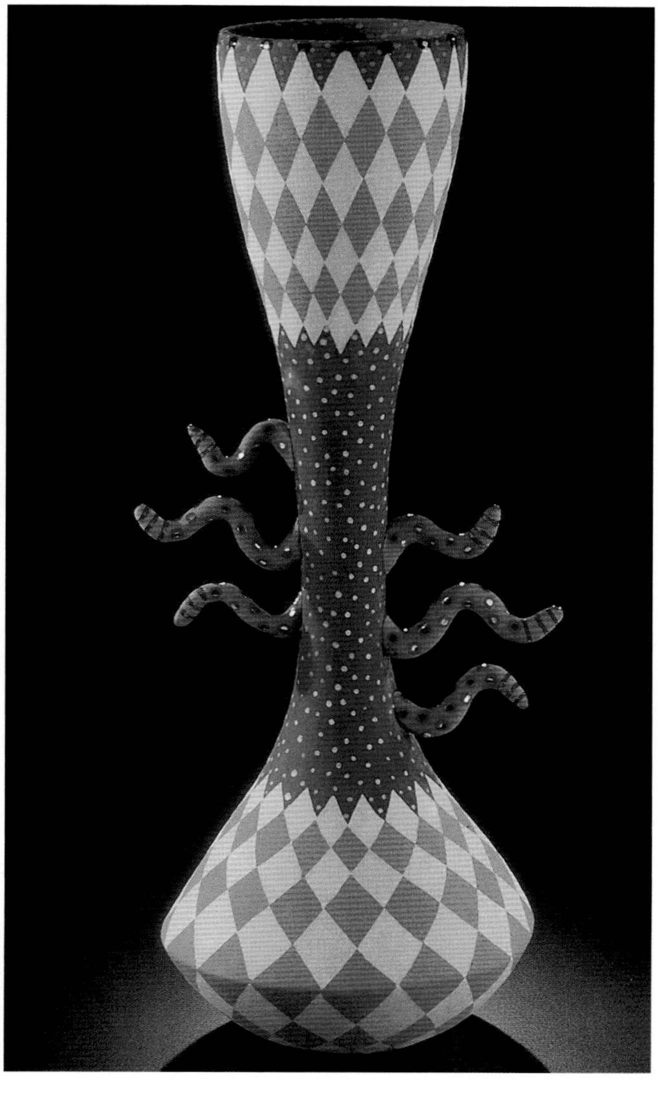

Above: **Robert Sanderson, *Walloped Teapot,*** 1996
4¼" x 6¾" x 4" (11 x 17.5 x 10.5 cm). Stoneware; thrown on modified Leach kick wheel, altered, lines made with piece of wood when leather hard, spout and rolled handle attached; wood fired for 24 hours to cone 11. Photo by John McKenzie

Left: **Judy Brater-Rose, *Vase,*** 1997
14" x 6" x 6" (35.5 x 15 x 15 cm). Stoneware; thrown, cut rim, added handles; surface etched and carved when leather hard; sponged and brushed layered overglazes; oxidation fired to cone 6.
Photo by Gary Heatherly

Bottom left: **Ron Meyers, *Casserole,*** 1997
6" x 9" x 9" (15 x 23 x 23 cm). Earthenware; thrown, with applied knob; drawn on and paddled; dipped into kaolin wash; salt fired to cone 04. Photo by Walker Montgomery

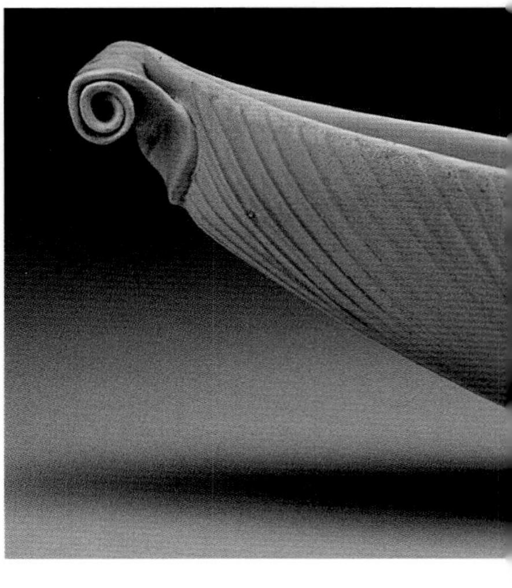

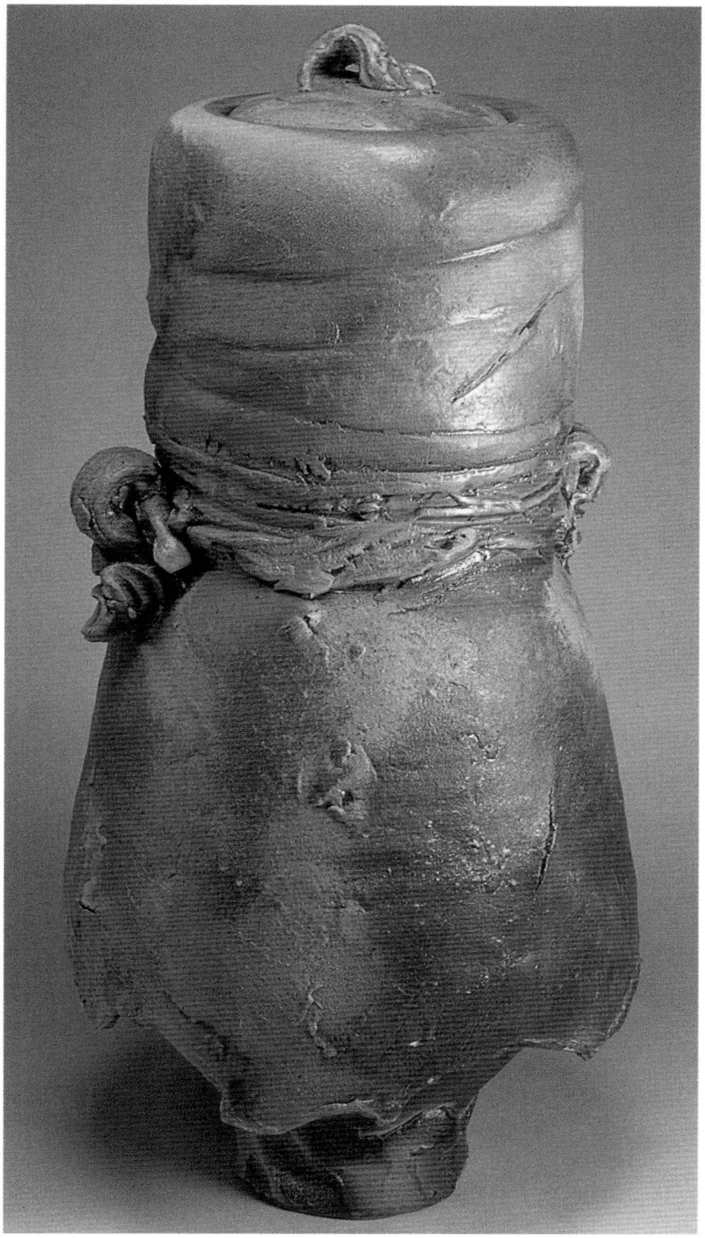

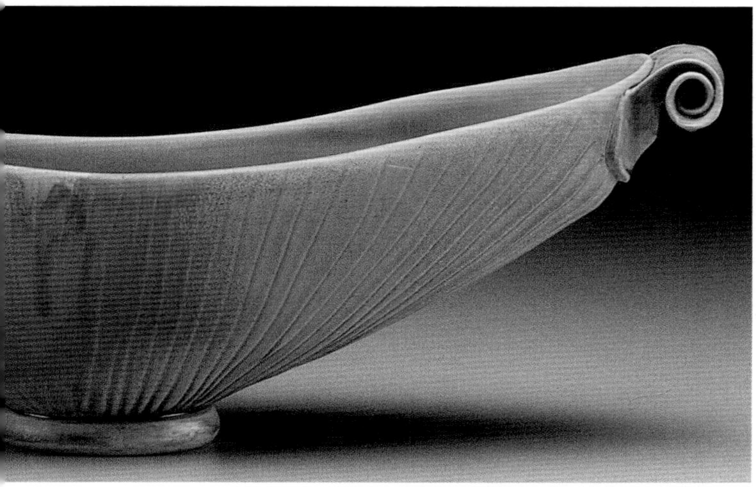

Above: **Don Reitz, *Lidded Vessel,*** 1997
42" x 18" (106.5 x 45.5 cm). Light stoneware with 20% grog; body thrown in four sections, sections joined when very stiff, lid thrown, body scraped when leather hard to remove throwing rings; sprayed with kaolin; fired in anagama kiln to cone 11 for five days. Photo by artist

Top left: **Ikuzi Teraki and Jeanne Bisson, *Chisel Cut Bowl,*** 1997
5½" x 8" x 5¼" (14 x 20 x 13.5 cm). Porcelain; thrown, trimmed, chisel-carved exterior; interior masked, slip applied to rim and exterior, mask removed, clear glaze applied to interior; bisque fired to cone 08; glaze fired in electric kiln to cone 6. Photo by artist

Center left: **Don Davis, *Double Neck Vase,*** 1997
Height: 9" (23 cm). Porcelain; thrown in three pieces, altered, and joined when leather hard; bisque fired to cone 06; bottom glazed with tape resist pattern; top sprayed with iron oxide solution and etched; glaze fired to cone 7, light reduction. Photo by Evan Bracken

Left: **Silvie Granatelli, *Oval Bowl,*** 1997
10" x 20" x 8" (25.5 x 51 x 20.5 cm). Porcelain; thrown and altered, faceted; dipped and sprayed glaze; fired in gas kiln to cone 10. Photo by Tim Barnwell

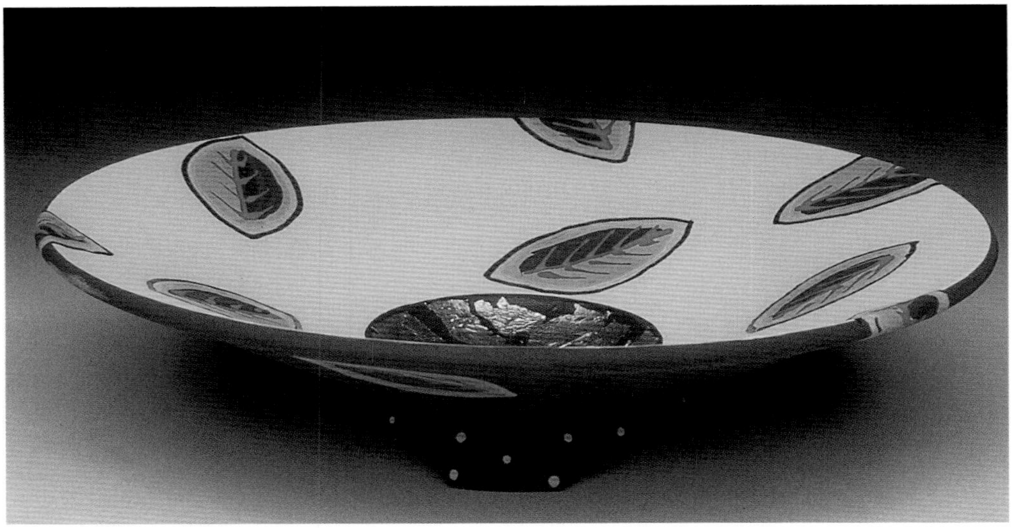

Left: **Barbara Mann,** ***Bowl,*** 1997
3" x 8" x 8" (7.5 x 20.5 x 20.5 cm). Earthenware; thrown; brushed and trailed matt glazes; oxidation fired to cone 06; copper leaf. Photo by Seth Tice-Lewis

Bottom left: **Allen Bales,** ***Genie Vase,*** 1997
33" x 14" x 14" (79 x 35.5 x 35.5 cm). Raku; thrown as two forms, foot trimmed on inverted leather form when leather hard, then joined; slip trailed, impressed with found objects, extruded and slab-rolled additions; bisque fired to cone 05; sprayed glaze; raku fired to cone 05, reduced in wood shavings; reoxidized and water-cooled. Photo by Linda Mooney Photography

Bottom right: **John Goodheart,** ***Brother Aquataine's Bucket,*** 1996
13" x 8" x 8" (33 x 20.5 x 20.5 cm). Red earthenware; thrown; multiple firings in electric kiln to cone 06 for sandpaper-like glaze surface; lid and copper accents added after glaze firings. Photo by Kevin Montague and Michael Cavanagh

CHAPTER TWO

Clay and Kilns

Jack Troy, ***Torqued Vase,*** 1995
7" x 5" x 5" (18 x 12.5 x 12.5 cm). Porcelain; after throwing, the form was torqued from the inside with a modified throwing stick, which the artist calls a "T-stick"; fired in anagama kiln

Clay and Kilns

In this chapter, we'll explore the different types of clay and kilns. Just as your choice of wheel will influence the work you do, so will the clay and kiln you use.

Clay

Clay is one of the most common, basic, yet complex and wonderful materials on the planet. Its elements are the same as those from which most of the earth is composed. It responds to and records the human touch like nothing else. Clay has preserved the footprints of man's prehistoric ancestors, and since man first discovered it, has been fashioned by hand into all manner of objects. When you pick up a piece of moist clay and shape it, you become an active participant in this ongoing, age-old relationship.

The Nature of Clay

Clay is the fortunate result of millions of years of natural processing. It starts out as mountain rock, and over the aeons is eroded, transported by water, sifted, and deposited elsewhere. During this process, many of the particles are ground to a very small size and become what we know as clay. As the particles move downhill, some are deposited in areas where the water transporting them has slowed down, but the largest clay deposits occur farther away, where rivers empty into estuaries. The geological process that creates clay is an ongoing one, and even today, nature creates more clay than man uses.

In its basic mineral state, pure clay (which doesn't exist in nature) is made up of alumina, silica, and water. The formula for the clay molecule is $Al_2O_3.2SiO_2.2H_2O$. In this state, clay would probably be pure white. Naturally occurring clays (many types exist), however, always contain impurities, from organic matter to small particles of other minerals. These impurities are what help to give each type of clay its individual qualities.

The color of a clay, for example, is usually a result of the impurities present in it, especially the amount and type of iron. Clays range from different shades of white through gray, tan, orange, brick red, and dark brown. The type of firing a clay undergoes also affects its color.

Moist clay's wonderful quality of flexibility is known as plasticity. Plastic clay can be shaped and will hold that shape until some force alters it. Clay's plasticity is in large part due to the fineness and plate-like shape of its particles. When they're wet, these flat particles slide over and support each other. Organic residue can also contribute to a clay's degree of plasticity by adding its own slippery qualities.

Letting a clay age increases its plasticity by allowing water to saturate its particles more thoroughly and by encouraging the growth of friendly bacteria. Too much plasticity results in a clay that feels too gummy and that is difficult to work with. A potter might refer to an overly plastic clay as "short."

The texture of a clay depends in part on the size of the majority of particles in it and can range from smooth to rough. A clay's visual texture is also affected by the presence of scattered particles of metals such as iron or manganese, which produce spots similar to freckles on the clay after it's fired.

The larger particles in any clay contribute what potters call "tooth." These particles strengthen plastic clay, and by tempering the slippery quality of the fine particles, make it easier to work with. The various-sized par-

ticles in a clay work together in the same way that stones of different sizes in a well-built stone wall fit together to make the wall stable. Adding some tooth to a short plastic clay can make it just right for throwing. Some clays naturally have a lot of tooth; these are referred to as "tough" clays. A clay with too much tooth feels sandy and is difficult to work with.

Clays also vary in their degree of porosity after firing. Clays fired to low temperatures will be somewhat porous and will still absorb water. A very porous clay wouldn't be a good choice for throwing utilitarian vessels unless it were fired with a sealing glaze of some kind.

Clay Bodies

A few clays are ready to dig up and use just as they are. These natural clay deposits provide exactly the right mix of materials for the potters who use them and require only minimal processing to remove rocks or sand that have settled with the clay particles. Historically, potteries developed near clay deposits, and the differences in the quality of the clays available in different areas influenced the type of ware that local potters made. Many potteries around the world still work in this traditional way, creating ware indigenous to their own areas and cultures.

Today, however, many large clay deposits are mined commercially, and the clay is bagged and shipped out for use in cosmetics, paints, and pottery. Because very few naturally occurring clays can be used straight from the ground, they're usually mixed, by the clay supplier or the individual potter, with one or more different types of clay and other ingredients to form what's known as a "clay body." Even potters who dig their own clay, for example, might mix a short clay with a tough clay to get the best clay body for throwing.

Potters can purchase an assortment of these premixed clays from clay suppliers, but many choose to mix their own from dry ingredients. Hundreds of clay-body formulas are available, and once you have a working knowledge of the various clays and ingredients, you can alter existing formulas or invent ones to suit your own particular needs. If you set out to mix your own clay bodies, the types of clay available for your use are kaolins (or china clays), ball, fire, and earthenware clays.

Kaolins or china clays are the purest and whitest and contain very little iron. They're also the least abundant, are not usually very plastic, have the highest fusion point (3272°F or 1800°C), and are the main ingredient in porcelain clay bodies.

Ball clays are fine-particled and very plastic, fuse at a lower temperature (2372°F or 1300°C) than kaolin and china clays, and when they're reduction fired in a kiln, turn slightly darker than the kaolins (usually light gray or tan). They make a good addition to a toothy or less plastic clay.

Fire clays tend to be relatively coarse, fuse at high temperatures (2732°F or 1500°C), and usually fire to a light gray or tan color. They vary in plasticity and are usually the main ingredient in stoneware clay bodies.

Earthenware clays are orange to brick red in color and because they contain the largest amount of impurities, especially iron, they fuse at the lowest temperature (1832°F or 1000°C) of any of the clays mentioned here. Earthenwares are the most abundant clays and have always been the most frequently used for pottery.

A clay formula consists of a list of ingredients by weight and will often call for specific brand-name clay types. Other ingredients might include silica, feldspar, sand, or grog. Grog is fired clay that has been crushed and sifted; it's available in a variety of particle sizes. Grog and sand add tooth to a clay body. Feldspar helps the clay to fuse at a lower temperature, and silica adds strength as well as glassiness to the body. Sometimes, a formula calls for an organic gum, which increases plasticity.

A typical formula for a stoneware clay body might include a fire clay for tooth, some ball clay for plasticity, perhaps a bit of red earthenware for color, and added feldspar to help the clay fuse and to help the melted glaze adhere better. A formula for a porcelain clay might include a kaolin or two (or an English china clay) and about 50% combined feldspar and flint. The beginning thrower will find that stoneware is easier to throw.

Mixing your own clay is vigorous work and requires some extra space and equipment. One simple way to mix clay is to weigh the dry ingredients, one at a time, into a container and mix them together. Next, you add water and mix again. Then the soupy mixture is spread out on a plaster slab and allowed to dry to a usable consistency. (Small test batches can easily be mixed in a bucket.) There are machines designed for mixing clay, and each kind makes use of a different clay-mixing method. Some methods are said to produce clay of superior quality, and some potters swear by and rigidly adhere to the methods they choose.

When one works well for you, and you achieve the desired results, it's wise to stick to it. While you're "sticking," however, trying an occasional experiment can also be enriching.

Clay that is right for throwing will be about one-third water by weight. The mood of the clay and its possibilities for throwing will change with the water content. Even a little too much water can make the clay difficult to work with; any form you try to throw, other than the simplest, won't stand up or hold its shape. Likewise, if the clay is too stiff, a thrower won't be able to do much with it. Different shapes require a slightly different degree of clay firmness, and different throwers prefer to work with clays of different consistencies. Potters must become acquainted with the qualities that a clay brings to the wheel, just as they must become familiar with the forms they choose to make with that clay.

If you're just beginning and are looking for some clay to throw, first be sure that the clay you get matches the temperature range to which it will be fired. Then ask your supplier for a good "throwing body" in a color you like.

Drying and Firing Clay

As clay dries, it passes through several stages. The one between moist and dry is known as "leather hard." Leather hardness begins when the clay loses the shine of wetness and continues through several stages until the clay is too stiff to dent when you push it firmly with your fingertip. Potters add moist clay pieces such as handles and spouts to a thrown pot when the pot is at the leather-hard stage because at this stage, the clay still hasn't shrunk from loss of moisture. Once a pot has passed the leather-hard stage, any moist clay added to it will crack off as it dries. Clay is also trimmed, carved, cut, or faceted when it's leather hard. You'll need some experience before you can distinguish the various stages of leather hardness and before you can tell how the clay will respond at each one.

"Bone-dry" clay is clay that has been completely air dried and is ready to be fired. ("Greenware" is the term used to refer to bone-dry pottery that hasn't been fired yet.) No additions are possible at the bone-dry stage, and because the clay is brittle, if you try to trim or carve it, the clay is likely to crack. I don't recommend finishing bone-dry clay by sanding or scraping it because doing so creates clay dust.

Clay shrinks as it dries and when it's fired in a kiln. A thrown piece will shrink in size by an average of 10%. About half of that shrinkage occurs during drying. The other half occurs when the piece is fired to vitrification (see the next page). You'll need to keep this in mind when you gauge the scale of the pieces that you want to make.

A group of fired cone packs, photographed in the kiln shed of Brad Tucker (Creedmoor, NC). Photo by Don Davis

Every clay body has an ideal cone-firing range (or range of temperatures) within which it will reach maturity—the desired density and hardness. To monitor the firing range within the kiln, you'll use small conical pieces of clay known as cones. These are available from clay suppliers and are formulated to melt and bend at specific kiln temperatures and to respond to the rate of heat increase. Some cones are freestanding and need no additional support; they're just placed on the kiln shelf. Others must be pressed into a coil of clay known as a "cone pack." It's a good idea to include several cones rated lower than the target cone and one rated above it to serve as a "guard" cone. Cones respond to firing in much the same way that clay and glazes do. By watching the cones as they begin to bend during firing, you can keep track of the temperature rise in your kiln. (See Appendix F on page 156 for a chart of cone-firing ranges.)

For the purposes of this book, when I refer to "low-fire" ranges, I'm referring to kiln temperatures ranging from cone 022 to cone 1. Mid-range firings run from cone 1 to 6, and high-fire ranges run from cone 6 to cone 12.

Bisque firing—a slow, low-temperature first firing (cone 08 to cone 04) that leaves the clay porous and ready for a glaze application—dramatically changes the clay. The chemical water that was bonded in it is driven off between 662°F and 1052°F (350°C and 500°C), and the clay will no longer slake back into its moist state when you immerse it in water. Firing green clay too quickly doesn't allow enough time for water to escape, which can cause the clay to explode.

Clay also goes through two more stages during bisque firing. One is the burn-off of carbon residue (clays vary in how much carbon they contain) at about 1652°F (900°C). The other is the phenomenon known as "quartz inversion," which occurs at 1063°F (573°C). During this stage the quartz particles in clay increase in size during heating and decrease in size during cooling. These phases of heating must be passed through slowly. If carbon isn't burned out successfully, bloating may occur when the clay reaches the point of vitrification, and if heating or cooling is too quick during quartz inversion, the ware will crack. (Quartz inversion occurs in any firing, so no firing should heat or cool too rapidly during this phase.)

Bisqued clay is in an ideal state for applying glazes or other surface treatments because even though it's hard, it's still absorbent. Whatever you apply to its surface will dry quickly. Any mistakes you make applying a glaze may also be washed off with water.

A glazed piece of bisqued ware is fired again, usually to a higher temperature in what's known as the glaze firing. (Even when I use little or no glaze on a piece, I'll sometimes refer to the final firing as the glaze firing.) Because bisqued ware is resistant to thermal shock, it can be heated up very quickly in the glaze firing.

Sometimes, glaze is applied to greenware and the piece is once-fired to the point of maturity. When this method is used, washing the glaze off is not an option.

Vitrified clay is clay that's been fired at temperatures high enough to fuse it to a point at which it will no longer absorb any water. (At this stage, the clay is very dense and stonelike.) After vitrification, the clay will no longer shrink. If clay is heated past the point of vitrification, it begins to break down and melt.

Recycling Clay

When thrown pieces collapse, you can wedge the moist clay and use it again. When you accumulate clay trimmings, clay slurry from throwing, and pieces of clay too dry to throw, you'll need to recycle them. A bucket filled about halfway with water can serve as your reclaim container. Place small pieces of leather-hard clay, such as leftovers from trimming, in the water; they'll slake down nicely. Larger pieces, such as pots, will only slake down if you let them dry completely first and break them into smaller pieces.

When the bucket is almost full, stir the contents vigorously with a power drill and mixer attachment. If you don't have access to a drill and mixer blade, stir the mixture as best you can with a stick or large whisk. Then add a scoop of dry, powdered fire clay or kaolin and blend it into the mix. This will help keep the recycled clay from being too plastic or short. Next, scoop the pudding-like clay onto a surface such as a plaster slab and let it dry enough to roll up and wedge. The clay will take a few days to get to this stage.

Storing Clay

To keep moist clay from drying out, place it in tightly sealed plastic buckets or bags. If your clay isn't tightly sealed, be sure to moisten it occasionally by covering it with a wet cloth and sprinkling the cloth with water.

Kilns

Whether you're ready to acquire a kiln of your own or are working in a studio where your work is fired for you, learning about the different kinds of kilns is a good idea. Different kilns produce very different effects on the clay forms and glazes fired in them, so the type of kiln you need will be determined by the type of work you want to produce.

Electric kilns are definitely the most convenient. A set of switches on the outside of the kiln controls the

Ben Owen III's gas-fired salt kiln (Seagrove, NC). The bricks that fill in the door during firing have been removed. Note the two holes visible on the sides of the open kiln above the burners. These are the "salt ports"—the openings through which the salt is added during firing. Photo by Don Davis

heating elements inside. These kilns are readily available from ceramic suppliers, and used models can often be purchased from individuals.

Moving and setting up an electric kiln is relatively easy—not much more involved than moving and setting up a kitchen stove—but do have a qualified electrician check the wiring and install any needed upgrades, circuit breakers, or plugs. Also be sure to place the kiln at a safe distance from walls and other objects (12 inches or 30.5 cm is usually sufficient).

Any clay or glaze will produce some harmful fumes when it's fired in a kiln. For this reason, I recommend setting up your kiln in an area separate from your work space. Motorized kiln vents are available and help remove fumes, as do exhaust fans in windows, but you still shouldn't spend any more time than necessary in the same small space as a kiln that's being fired. The heat given off may also be unbearable in warm weather.

Electric kilns come in a range of sizes. I recommend an 8- or 10-cubic-foot (.22 or .28 m^3) kiln for anyone who plans to throw pots regularly. (Smaller kilns won't hold as much ware.) Firing a kiln that isn't entirely full just isn't efficient, so pieces to be fired are stacked on removable refractory kiln shelves, which come in different sizes to fit different kilns. These shelves can be arranged on posts of different heights.

Most electric kilns are loaded from the top, through a hinged door that can be propped open. Larger kilns, as well as models that open from the side, are available. These cost considerably more than smaller or top-loading kilns and may also require heavier wiring.

Electric kilns are best used to produce oxidation firings—ones during which a normal amount of oxygen is present inside the kiln. This interior kiln atmosphere affects the quality of the ware produced. In reduction firings, which are usually done in non-electric kilns, the oxygen levels inside the kiln are deliberately reduced in order to produce different effects on the ware (see pages 147-149 for details).

Gas-fired kilns can produce either reduction firings or oxidation firings. Installing and firing them is considerably more complex than installing and firing electric kilns. You'll need professional help hooking up the gas, and if the burners have forced-air blowers attached, you may need an electrician, too. Placing a gas-fired kiln in a separate, well-ventilated area is absolutely essential. A separate kiln shed is ideal.

Shiho Kanzaki, Japanese potter, stoking his wood-fired anagama kiln. Photo courtesy of Dick Lehman

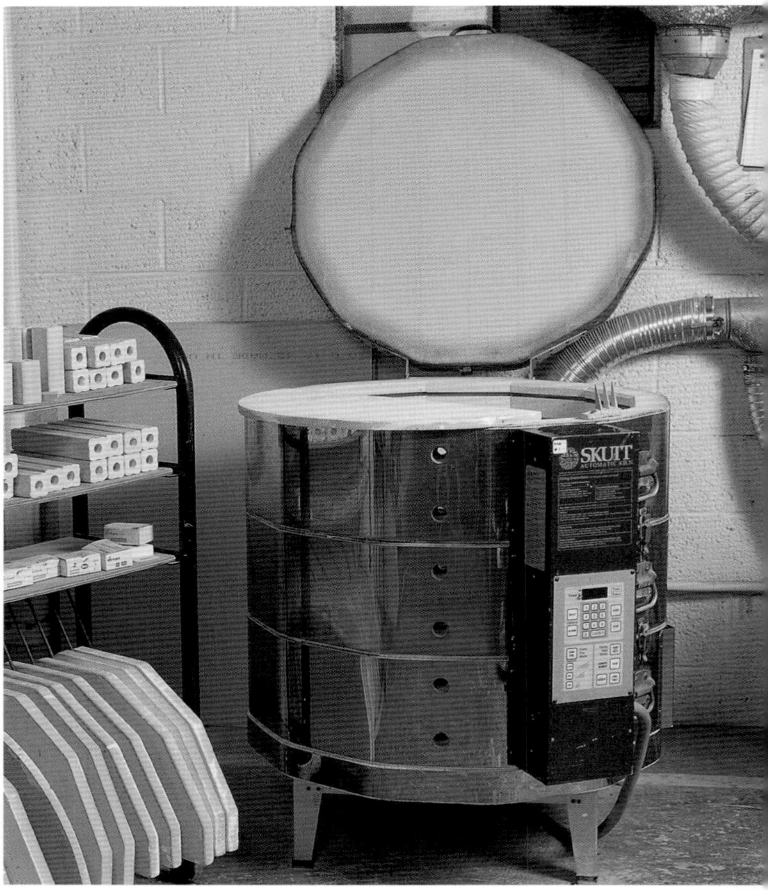

An electric kiln at Odyssey Center for Ceramic Arts (Asheville, NC). Note the kiln furniture (posts and shelves) to the left of the kiln. Photo by Evan Bracken

Tom Gray's gas-fired catenary arch kiln (Seagrove, NC). The two burners enter from the back, and the exit flue and chimney (or stack) are also on the back. Photo by Don Davis

Additional fire safety precautions will come into play. (You're working with real fire in a gas kiln, and these kilns are usually fired to higher temperatures than electric kilns.)

High-temperature gas-fired kilns also require a much larger financial investment than electric kilns. Many potters build their own and customize their sizes and configurations to suit their own needs. If you want to build your own gas-fired kiln, helpful books on the subject are available. I also recommend taking a kiln-building workshop if you can, and seeking help from an experienced kiln builder when you begin to build your own.

Other types of kilns include raku, wood-fired, salt, and primitive pit firing setups. (You'll find more about their different effects on surface treatments on pages 147-149.) Again, excellent books are available on kilns and firing. For help setting up one of these kilns, I also recommend attending workshops or seeking out potters who work in these areas.

Somalian potters arranging their pots for firing. The larger pots are placed on the bottom and wood is placed around each one. Prior to firing, the pots are thoroughly dried in the sun, with burning charcoal placed inside each one. Photo by John Selker, courtesy of Laurie Childers

Marian Davis, cleaning the bottom of a pot while unloading a gas-fired car kiln. Photo by Don Davis

Top left: **Steven Glass, *Bottle,*** 1997
11" x 7" x 7" (28 x 18 x 18 cm). White stoneware; thrown; painted slips, sgraffito, glazed; oxidation glaze fired to cone 7. Photo by Mike Pocklington

Above: **M. Oya (Ichizen, Japan), *Untitled,*** 1985
Height: 8" (20.5 cm). Thrown and paddled; wood fired in anagama kiln. Photo courtesy of Glenn Rand

Bottom left: **Daniel Seagle** (1805-1867), ***Jug***
Lincoln County, NC. Stoneware. Seagle was a prolific potter who brought high standards of craftsmanship to his work. He was also one of the first Southern potters to switch from earthenware to alkaline-glazed stoneware. Photo courtesy of Sid Oakley and the Museum of American Pottery

Right: **Karen Karnes, *Winged Vessel,*** 1989
Stoneware; wood fired. Photo courtesy of Garth Clark Gallery, New York, NY

Bottom left: **David Pinto, *Best Foot Forward,*** 1997
15" x 9" x 9" (38 x 23 x 23 cm). Stoneware; thrown closed form altered on wheel by pushing in base; after stiffening, sculpted feet and side ribs created; at leather-hard stage, bases added to feet and finish detailed with scraper; wood fired in anagama kiln, light salt, to cone 11-12. Photo by Paul Stopie and artist

Bottom right: **George McCauley, *Covered Jar,*** 1994
26" x 11" x 11" (66 x 28 x 28 cm). Earthenware; thrown, altered off the wheel, faceted while still soft; terra sigillata applied; bisque fired; iron wash applied and sponged off; barium glaze; soda fired to cone 01

Left: **Colleen Black-Semelka,** ***Giraffe Pattern Vase,*** 1997
9" x 13" x 13" (23 x 33 x 33 cm). Stoneware; thrown, altered by tapping sides with wooden paddle when leather hard; white slip applied to greenware; bisque fired to cone 06; brushed raku glaze; raku fired to cone 08, reduced in leaves and newspaper. Photo by Seth Tice-Lewis

Bottom left: **Ben Owen III,** ***Egg Vase—Oribe,*** 1997
6" x 4" x 4" (15 x 10 x 10 cm). Porcelain; thrown; combed surface; wood-fired to cone 12. Photo by David Ramsey

Bottom right: **Nathaniel Dixon (1827-1863),** ***Stoneware Storage Jar***
Height: 14" (35.5 cm). This jar is a good example of traditional American salt-glazed ware. Photo courtesy of Sid Oakley and the Museum of American Pottery

CHAPTER THREE

Beginning To Throw

John Tilton, *Gourd Covered Jar,* 1997
10½" x 5½" x 5½" (26.5 x 14 x 14 cm). Porcelain; thrown in one piece, except lid; force-dried to stiffen while working; layered matt crystalline glazes applied between multiple reduction firings to cone 10. Photo by artist

Beginning To Throw

In this chapter, I'll describe the basic steps of throwing a cylinder—a multistage process that beginning throwers will need to master before they can tackle throwing and shaping more complex forms. These basic descriptions may also prove helpful to those of you who have been throwing for a few years.

As you read, keep in mind that there are many variations on throwing techniques. Some potters, for example, throw standing up, often because the standing position is easier on their backs. Hand positions for centering and opening clay vary widely, too. The methods described in this book are fairly common, but if you discover other effective ways to handle clay as you throw it, by all means use them.

Starting Tips

- The instructions in this book are based on the assumption that the wheel is turning counterclockwise. (Most North Americans and Europeans throw this way.)
- Because the work photographed for this book was thrown on bats, the instructions assume that you'll be working with bats, too. If you're throwing directly on a wheel head, just ignore the references to bats.
- At any stage of the throwing process, you should always steady yourself when you can by bracing your hands, fingers, and arms against each other or against something else. If you're centered, steady, and stable, the clay will come along with you.
- Whenever you plan to work with clay, start by making sure that anything your clay will touch, including your hands, are clean and free of dried clay and other materials. Lumps and bumps in moist clay make it difficult to work with and can cause cracking as the piece dries.

Preparing the Clay

If you're new to throwing and have access to a clay supplier, treat yourself to a fresh bag of de-aired clay. This clay won't need much preparation. Slice off a 3-inch-thick (7.6 cm) slab from the block and divide it into four equal pieces, each about 1½ to 2 pounds (.7 to .9 kg) in weight. Each piece should fit comfortably between your cupped hands. (After you've had some practice, you'll be able to work with larger pieces.)

Even de-aired, bagged clay can be inconsistent in its moisture content, especially if the bag has been sitting around for a while. Over time, the moisture in unused clay migrates outward. To create shock waves that will redistribute the moisture, pat each piece of clay by sending it vigorously back and forth from one hand to the other several times.

Place the four balls of clay on a work surface near your wheel and wrap them with plastic to prevent them from drying out as they wait to be thrown. Also make sure that all your clay is covered tightly or placed in a sealed bag whenever it's not in use. As soon as clay is exposed to the air, it begins to dry out.

If you've hand-mixed your clay, if you're recycling clay from a collapsed pot, or if you're using clay that's been uncovered long enough to begin drying out, you'll need to wedge it before throwing it. Large pieces of clay for large forms must also be wedged. Wedging—a process similar to kneading bread—serves two purposes. It removes trapped air in the clay, and it redistributes the moisture evenly. I wedge all my clay (even fresh, bagged clay) because I like to get the feel of it before I start throwing it.

You'll need a very sturdy surface for wedging. Potters have used everything from old gristmill wheels and wood or cement floors to plaster slabs for this purpose. My own wedging table consists of a thick, cast-plaster slab that's covered with a piece of canvas. Any sturdy, flat surface will do.

If you've never wedged before, start with a chunk of clay that you can hold comfortably in your cupped hands. Place it on the wedging surface, and using Photo 1 as a guide, lean forward and push against it,

1

applying equal pressure with the heels of both hands. Then, using your fingers, roll the clay back toward you. Repeat this process for several minutes, rocking forward and backward as you do. Be very careful not to fold the clay back on itself as you roll it toward you, as the folds will trap air. Don't push too far forward, either. When you extend the clay out too far, it's flattened too much, and you're more likely to trap air as you roll it back. To prevent the clay from spreading out too much laterally as you wedge, also be sure to apply some inward force with your fingers and palms. When you use this method, your wedged clay should look like the piece of clay shown to the left in Photo 2. The clay will have symmetrical spirals on both sides.

2

After completing about fifty wedging strokes, shorten the length of each stroke. Then roll the clay back toward you, shaping it into a ball or cone before taking it to the wheel. (Note that the amount of wedging required will vary according to the condition of your clay.)

One variation on simple wedging—a variation that's necessary on large chunks of clay—includes a slight twisting motion each time you push the clay forward. This twist creates a characteristic spiral effect, which appears on only one side of the clay. (The larger lump of clay shown in Photo 2 provides a good example.) After completing about fifty strokes with this wedging method, roll the clay into a cone shape, with the spirals on the bottom. Then, to smooth out the spirals, roll the bottom of the cone in a circular pattern on the wedging surface. The clay is now ready to take to the wheel and throw.

Another way to de-air clay and redistribute moisture, especially with large chunks of clay, is to cut the clay into slices and recombine them. Start by using a cut-off wire to cut a slice from the chunk. Then slam this slice down hard on a sturdy work surface. Cut another slice and slam it down on top of the first. Continue until all the clay has been sliced and stacked in this manner. Then repeat these steps two or three times.

(To simplify this process, instead of using a hand-held cutoff wire, stretch a wire tightly from the front of your wedging table to a board fastened above and behind the table and secure the ends in place.) Clay prepared this way is usually also wedged afterwards.

Sometimes, your clay may be too wet to throw the form you have in mind. (Some forms require clay that is soft; others require clay that is stiffer.) To help wet clay dry out a bit after wedging, shape it into a solid cylinder, bend the cylinder, and allow the resulting clay arch to sit uncovered on a table top (Photo 3).

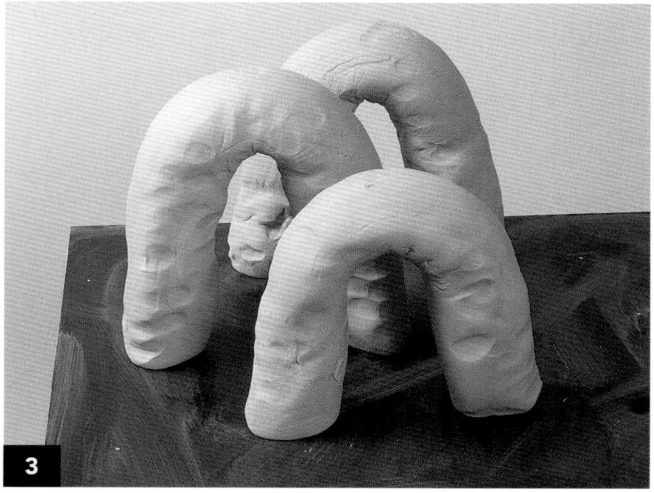

3

An arched cylinder of clay will dry evenly because it doesn't have any corners or edges that might lose moisture more rapidly than thicker portions. The exposed surface will always dry more than the interior, of course, so check the clay every hour or two. When the surface has stiffened somewhat, rewedge the clay, and either let it stiffen some more or, if it feels ready to throw, take it to the wheel.

Centering the Clay

In order to throw a symmetrical form, your clay must be coaxed to the exact center of your bat. Centering is simply a matter of applying even, consistent pressure to the clay as it spins on the wheel. The center is the point of least resistance, and your job is to help the clay get there. Centering does take practice, but if you stay focused and patient, the process will come. Those who are determined to throw will throw.

You'll find that centering is easier to learn if you remember a couple of important tips. Use your entire body as a unit, not just your hands; and use more leverage than muscle. Remember, too, that centering goes beyond mere mechanics. The process can require from the potter a mental state of centeredness as well.

Before you start, take the time to read the instructions that follow. You may also want to make a few "dry runs" by practicing the hand, arm, and torso motions before you place any clay on the wheel.

When you're ready to start, if your wheel has an absorbent plaster bat, moisten the bat by wiping it with a damp sponge. Also moisten the ball of clay that you plan to center. The moisture will help the clay stick to the bat as you work. (Dry plaster will suck moisture out of your clay, and the clay will pop off as the wheel turns.) If your wheel has a nonabsorbent bat or if you're throwing on the wheel head, don't moisten the bat or wheel head. Wet clay won't stick to a wet, nonabsorbent surface.

Plunk the ball of clay firmly down onto the bat, as close to the center as possible. With the wheel turning very slowly, use both hands at once to push the ball firmly on opposite sides a few times. This will help move the clay into the center of the bat and stick solidly to it (Photo 4).

Wet your hands by dipping them into a bucket of water. (The temperature of the water is only important for your own personal comfort.) Wet the clay by dipping your sponge into the bucket and using the wet sponge to dribble water over the clay (Photo 5).

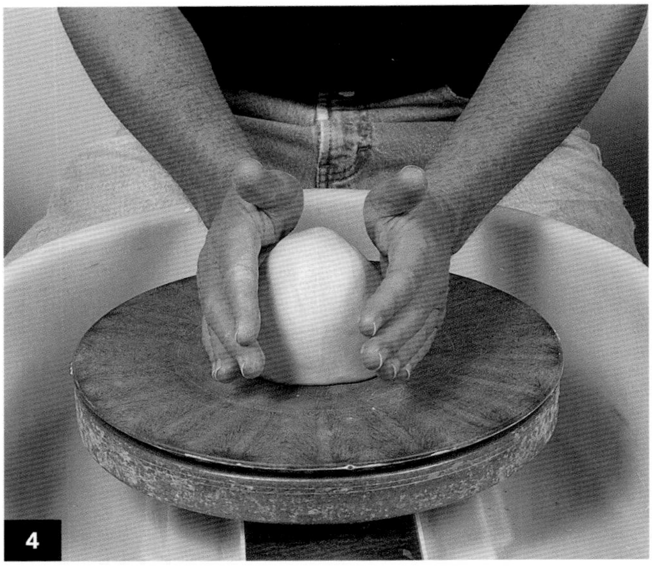
4

5

The instructions that follow cover two basic methods for centering clay while you're in a sitting position. One is to apply equal pressure through both arms and hands. With the other method, your left arm and hand are used as a lever, with your right fist behind your left hand. No matter which method you use, the force you exert will be forward and slightly down into the clay and will shape the ball of clay into a dome. This is the shape you'll need to center for any cylindrical form. For a bowl or spherical shape, you'll center a shape that looks more like a doorknob, and for a plate, you'll need to center a low disk shape. (You'll find instructions for making these last two shapes in the projects themselves.)

Centering Method #1

To get some sense of the motions required with this centering method, hold both hands straight out in front of you, touching them together at the heels, with your thumbs up and your fingers slightly apart. Then bend your arms at about 90 degrees at the elbows and brace your upper arms and elbows firmly against the sides of and slightly in front of your torso. Without bending your elbows, lean forward from the waist a few times, toward the bat. When you center the clay, you'll use your body in the same fashion.

Increase the speed of the wheel; it should be turning faster during centering than at any other time during the throwing process. Different potters work at slightly different speeds; use one that's comfortable for you. If you're using a kick wheel without an attached motor, kick quickly and let the wheel spin freely while you engage the clay. If you're working on a motorized kick wheel, engage the motor while you're centering. If you're using an electric wheel that allows you to set the speed, do so, and take your foot off the pedal if there is one. Plant both feet firmly on the ground to help stabilize your body.

Next, lean forward until your hands are pushing firmly against the clay. Depending on how you're seated, you may want to brace your arms against your legs for extra stability. The clay will start centering as it takes on the shape between your hands (Photo 6).

6

As you're centering, whenever your hands cease to slip freely on the clay, remove them slowly and smoothly, moisten them again, and rewet the clay before continuing. Keep your movements smooth; taking your hands off the clay too quickly will knock it off center. Also remember to stay braced and to use your whole body as a unit for leverage. Don't let your arms move back as you lean into the clay; they must convey the force of your body to it. You'll probably be surprised by how much force is required to center the clay. Lean into it!

Many newcomers to throwing find it difficult to know when their clay is centered and end up centering and decentering it several times without realizing it. ("Is it centered? Is it centered?") When clay is centered, it doesn't wobble on the spinning wheel. After some practice, you'll develop a tactile as well as visual ability to tell when the clay is centered. To help develop this tactile sense, try closing your eyes as you work. Removing all visual stimuli encourages you to depend on touch and even on sound.

Centering Method #2

The second method for centering clay while you're seated automatically prevents your arms from being forced backward as you move forward against the clay. With this method, one of your arms is well braced against your body (Photo 7).

7

To position yourself, tuck your left elbow just inside the front of your left hip. Extend your left forearm straight out in front of your body, with your fingers straight out and your thumb up. Now lean forward as if you were a lever, bringing the heel of your left hand forward to engage the clay. Your leaning body will exert force to the clay through this arm and hand. Place your right fist behind your left thumb and use it to help your left hand as it presses forward. As you center the clay, your left thumb will gradually move down on top of it, in order to prevent it from rising too high. Be careful not to let your thumb make a hole in the clay at this stage.

Don't forget to remoisten your hands and the clay as necessary.

Opening the Clay

After the clay is centered, opening comes next. This is a two-step process. The opening method described in this section is only one of many, but whatever method you use, the basic process is the same. During opening, you'll always be pushing the clay from the inside out, never from the outside in.

As you open the clay, remember to keep your hands and the clay moist. When excess water collects at the bottom of the opened clay, squeeze out your sponge and hold it lightly against the bottom to absorb the water.

Opening (Stage #1)

Before starting, reduce the wheel speed a little. Then let your left thumb glide on top of the clay, with its tip right at the center. (After you've had some experience, you'll be able to identify the exact center of the clay by touch; it's the place that offers the least resistance.) Now, keeping the fingers of your right hand together, place your middle right finger directly on top of your left thumbnail (Photo 8). Your fingers should act together whenever you work with clay on a wheel, especially during opening, so remember not to separate them.

8

Next, push your left thumb down into the clay and press down until the clay under your thumb is about ⅛ to ¼ inch (3 to 6 mm) thick, or as thick as you'd like the bottom of your thrown piece to be (Photo 9). As you do this, keep the tip of your thumb in the center of the clay and let the fingers of your left hand glide along on the outer wall. When you're finished, the opening will be bowl shaped.

9

Checking the thickness of the clay at the bottom is easy. First stop the wheel. Then push a needle tool straight down into the center of the opening, right down to the bat (Photo 10). Slide one finger down the needle until it touches the clay. Keeping that finger pressed against the needle, lift the tool up. The distance from the tip of the tool to your fingertip will be the thickness of the clay.

10

Opening sometimes pushes the clay off center. When you reset the rim you'll even it up again.

Opening (Stage #2)

The second stage of opening (in this case, for any flat-bottomed cylindrical form) involves extending the opening by moving the clay outward. To begin, place the fingers of your left hand inside the opening, with the tip of the middle finger at its center. Now place the right hand on top of the left and, with the bent fingers of both hands working together, pull the clay outward (Photo 11). Let your left thumb glide along the outside; don't exert any pressure with it. As you pull out, be sure to maintain the thickness of the clay at the bottom by keeping your fingers moving on a plane parallel to the bat. When you separate a thrown piece from a nonabsorbent bat or the wheel head, the cutoff wire you use will claim a very thin slice of clay from the bottom, so avoid making the bottom too thin.

11

12

When you've finished, the interior bottom of the clay may be uneven. To eliminate any variations in thickness and to level out the bottom, push a damp sponge downward against the turning clay (Photo 12).

Resetting

The two goals of resetting are to angle the wall of the opened clay slightly inward and to recenter it if necessary. You'll always reset the clay after you open it and after each "pull" that you make. (Pulling is described in the next section.)

The wheel should continue to rotate at your opening speed. Place the fingers of your left hand inside the opened clay, with your left thumb on the outer wall. This hand will serve only as a support. Now, holding a moist sponge between the thumb and fingers of your right hand, push the clay at the rim inward against your left hand (Photo 13). (I hold my sponge so that it covers the middle three fingers of my hand, so I'm actually pushing the clay with the sponge.) Adjust the pressure you apply and direct it as necessary toward the areas of the clay that need to be centered.

13

As with all the stages of throwing, there are several other ways to reset the clay. One is to place the palms of both hands on the outside and use them to push inward.

Pulling a Cylinder

Pulling is the gradual process of drawing the clay up to form the wall of the piece and is a process that's repeated several times with each form you throw. As you learn to pull, it's wise to remember that the centrifugal force of the spinning wheel will cause the clay to move outward as well as upward unless you convince the clay to do otherwise. In effect, every thrown piece wants to become a bowl, especially when the wheel is rotating too quickly. (If the wheel is spinning much too quickly, pieces of your pot may end up sprayed around the room!) To pull a cylindrical form that doesn't flare out at the top, you must counteract this force by keeping the top of the cylinder slightly narrower in diameter than the bottom.

First, slow the wheel down to pulling speed. (This speed varies from potter to potter.) Then use your sponge to wet both the inner and outer surfaces of the opened clay.

Before you make the first pull, read the following instructions and tips carefully. They'll help you coordinate your movements.

To make the first pull (three or four may be required to create this cylinder), start by placing the fingers of your left hand inside and at the bottom right-hand side of the opened clay. Then push outward with the tip of your middle finger to establish a small groove at the bottom of the clay wall. Next, place the middle finger of your right hand on the outside of the clay, resting it on the bat. (As you can see in Photo 14, I pull while holding a sponge in my outer hand. Doing so is a matter of convenience. When the clay needs rewetting, the sponge is right where I need it—in my hand. If you find that holding the sponge in this way is uncomfortable, just set it down before pulling.)

Now move both hands—and the groove in the clay—upward simultaneously. By pushing in with your outer finger at the very base of the clay as you start the pull, you'll avoid being left with too much excess clay at the bottom of your finished piece.

Each pull you make will move the clay gradually upward (Photos 15, 16, 17, and 18). Pulling will also add water to the clay and will soften it. Too much water will eventually result in clay fatigue. When this happens, the clay becomes very difficult to work with. You're better off starting over with another ball of clay than continuing to pull clay that's too wet. Your eventual goal should be to pull your cylinder to its full height in no more than two or three pulls.

14

Pulling Tips

■ As you start the pull, make sure your inner finger starts pushing out at the very bottom. This will create as close to a right angle as possible at the interior bottom of the form and will help you avoid making a bottom-heavy cylinder. With any thrown piece, the more the inside and outside shapes reflect each other, the better balanced the piece will be.

■ When you begin a pull, your outer finger should be slightly below your inner finger, but as your hands move up, your outer finger should gradually pull even with the inner one. By the time you approach the end of the pull, your fingers should be on the same horizontal plane.

■ Let the other fingers of each hand support the finger making the pull and keep your hands steady by bracing them against each other whenever possible.

■ Pull up at a speed that synchronizes with the speed of your wheel. Getting a feel for this will come with practice and is essential to successful throwing. You'll

15

16

17

18

know you've mastered pulling when the visible finger grooves in the clay spiral upward evenly, much like the grooves on a record.

■ The pressure you exert should be very firm but steady and should be greater at the bottom of the pull than at the top. As your fingers approach the top of the cylinder, reduce the pressure considerably and release the clay gently when you're through, or you'll knock the growing cylinder off center. A well-pulled clay wall tapers from slightly thicker at the bottom to thinner toward the top and then thickens again at the rim.

■ Sometimes, when you've applied uneven pressure during a pull or the cylinder is off center, one side of your thrown piece will be thicker than the other, and the rim will be uneven. Don't expect your first efforts to be perfect; throwing takes practice! Grab some more clay and try again.

■ When making the first pull, some potters prefer to use their knuckles instead of their fingers.

After each pull, reset the rim as you did after opening to eliminate any wobbliness (Photos 19 and 20). Also use your sponge to mop out any standing water in the bottom of the piece. Then wet the inside and outside walls before pulling up again.

19

20

Cutting the Rim

Once you're a proficient thrower, you'll usually be able to skip this step because the rims of your thrown forms will be even and level. In the meantime, cutting off the uneven portion of a rim is a technique that's sure to come in handy. You'll also use it when you've "necked in" a piece to form a smaller opening, which often results in an uneven rim.

First, make sure your fingers and the clay are wet enough to allow your fingers to glide smoothly. Place the fingers of your left hand inside the form, toward the very top of the wall, and allow your left thumb to ride along the outside. Holding a needle tool in your right hand, rest the shaft of the needle on your left thumb, with its point aimed straight ahead.

Take a deep breath. Exhale. Now, with the wheel spinning at pulling speed (fairly slowly), push the point of the needle through the clay, pivoting the tool on your thumb to rest against the index finger of your left hand, on the inside of the pot (Photo 21). Holding your fingers and the needle tool steady, carefully lift the cut rim away (Photo 22) and set it aside. Then use the sponge or a chamois and your fingers to smooth the cut edges.

21

22

A Review

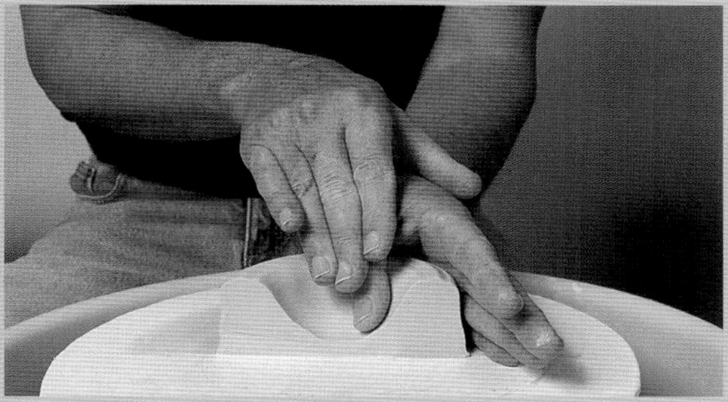

After centering, the clay is opened by placing the fingers of the right hand over the left thumb and pushing down. Note the slope of the interior wall at this stage.

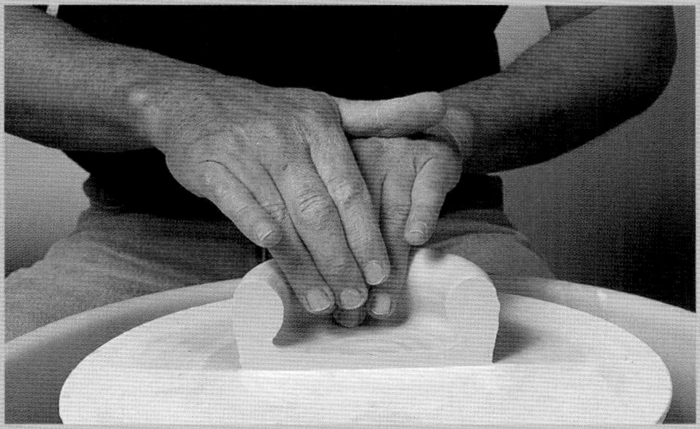

The bottom is then expanded and flattened by using the fingers of both hands to open the clay by pressing it outward.

After sponging the bottom and resetting the rim, the first pull is started. The middle finger of the left hand pushes outward as the middle finger of the right hand pushes inward. Remember to start the groove with both fingers positioned as far down as possible.

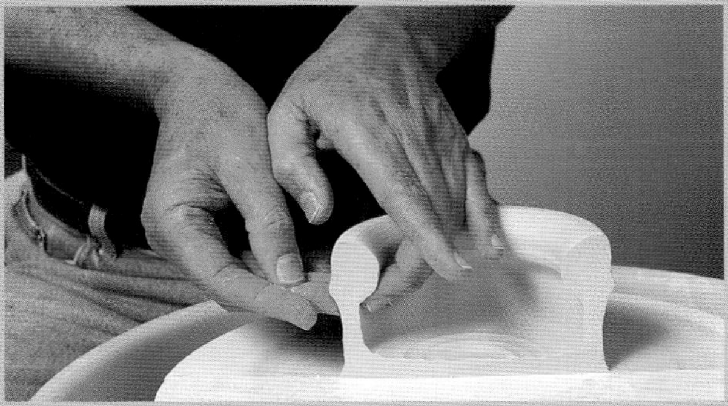

As the fingers reach the middle of the first pull, they're almost aligned on the same horizontal plane.

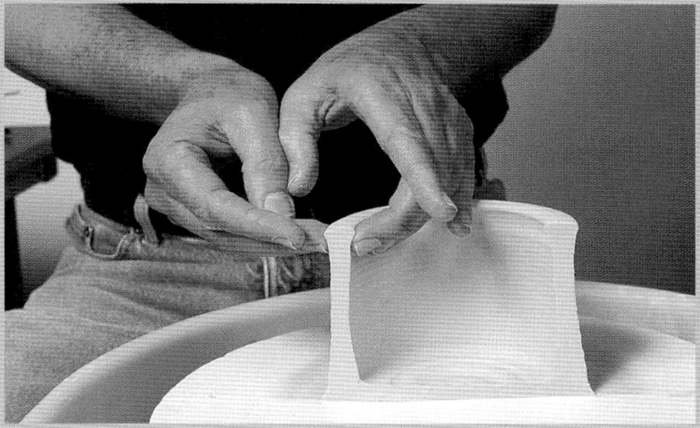

At the top of the first pull, the fingers are directly opposite one another, and the pressure is eased before they're released from the clay. Note that the rim of the cylinder is thicker than its wall.

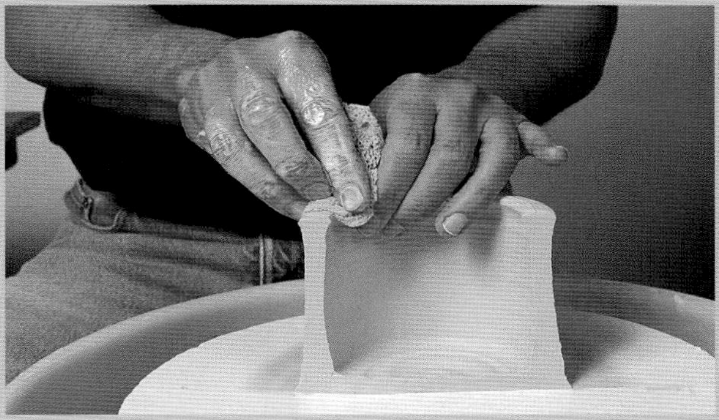

The rim is reset in order to even it out and recenter it.

The cylinder wall is gradually thinned as the clay is pulled up again.

The final pull establishes the final height of the form. Note the taper of the wall thickness.

Your thrown cylinder will probably have some excess clay at the base. To remove this clay, first draw a cutting stick down the outer surface, at the bottom of the form, following an imaginary line that represents the desired contour, until the tip of the tool touches the bat (Photo 23). The wheel should be turning slowly as you do this. The excess clay that you've cut away will form a ring around the form.

23

Next, while the wheel continues to turn, hold the tip of the cutting stick slightly above the cut and trickle water down it. The water will run down into the groove between the base of your form and the clay ring, and will help keep the ring from sticking back onto the form as you remove it. Now use the cutting tool to cut the ring loose from the bat (see Photos 136, 137, and 138 on page 120). This technique can come in very handy when you're throwing spherical forms because the cut ring on a spherical form is especially likely to reattach itself to the piece as you try to cut it away. Trimming the excess clay in this fashion can also eliminate the need for any further trimming on flat-bottomed pieces.

Cutting the Form from the Wheel

If you're working with a plaster bat, skip this step, as the plaster will absorb enough water from the bottom of your piece to allow you to pop the piece loose when it has dried a bit; you won't have to cut it free first. Cutting off is only necessary when you've thrown the clay on a nonabsorbent surface such as a plastic bat or the wheel head and should be done immediately after throwing.

To help guide the cutoff wire that you'll use to free the form, as the wheel turns, mark a small groove at the base of the wall (Photo 24). Then stop the

24

wheel. Hold one end of a cutoff wire in each hand, pull the wire taut, and place it on the far side of the throwing surface. Using the thumb of each hand to hold the wire flat against the throwing surface, pull the wire toward you and under the piece to release it (Photo 25). (I've seen potters start at the near side of the pot and pass the wire under it, toward the far side.) Using the groove made by your stick helps the wire make a cleaner cut. Be sure to hold the wire tightly down on the bat as you pull it. If the wire is too long and awkward, I sometimes wrap it around my hand to shorten it. If you do this, be careful not to let the wire pinch your hand.

If you've thrown the piece on a bat rather than on the wheel head, you may want to leave your form on the bat for a few hours after cutting it free so the clay will firm up a bit before you handle it. Carefully remove the bat and form from the wheel and set them aside. If you haven't used much water during throwing and the form is fairly stable, you may be able to remove it from the bat immediately. Hold it gingerly between the palms of both hands and lift it onto a ware board or move it with pot lifters.

Another way to remove the form from a nonabsorbent surface is to create a film of water next to it before cutting it free. As you bring the cutoff wire under the form, glide the pot over the film of water and onto a ware board placed right next to the wheel head or bat. Then set the board and form aside.

25

Removing the form from the bat as quickly as possible frees the bat for the next use. (If you're throwing directly on the wheel head, you must remove the pot before you can throw another.)

Finishing the Bottom

The bottoms of pots are just as important as any other part and need to receive their fair share of attention. Flat-bottomed pieces, including mugs, pitchers, vases, and some bowls, may be finished by simply rounding off their bottom edges. (At the leather-hard stage, a rough edge will still be soft to the touch, but after firing, any rough or sharp edges will be very unpleasant.)

When the piece is leather hard, remove it from the bat. (If you've thrown your cylinder on a plastic bat and it's stuck, cut it off again with the wire. If the piece is stuck onto a plaster bat, carefully work a long, flat spatula under it as it turns slowly on the wheel.) Now run one finger or your thumb around the bottom edge to remove any stray bits of clay. Next, position the piece at an angle of about 45 degrees on a clean work surface. Then roll the piece around on its bottom edge (Photo 26). Run one finger or a thumb around the edge again to make sure that it's no longer sharp. Then tap the bottom of the piece lightly with your fingers to push it up slightly. Unless you do this, the bottom may bulge out as the clay becomes bone dry, resulting in a pot that rocks.

26

If you find that you've distorted the pot or that your fingers have left unwanted dents in it, the clay wasn't yet dry enough to handle. Monitoring the degree of dryness is one of the most challenging aspects of working with clay and will be critical when you're trimming or adding handles, spouts, feet, and other parts to a thrown piece.

After finishing the bottom, let the cylinder dry, uncovered.

Moving On

Learning to throw on the potter's wheel requires developing some new types of mind/body coordination. The process will probably seem awkward at first but, as with any new endeavor, practice and time will eventually make it begin to feel natural. When you watch accomplished potters turn graceful shapes on the wheel, remember that they've no doubt been throwing for many years.

Even if you don't plan to put in the time required to become a pro, learning to work on the wheel can be a rewarding experience. Start by throwing cylinders until you've gained some confidence in your skills and are more familiar with your clay and wheel. Then move on to the projects in the next chapter.

Top left: **Ole Morten Rokvam,** ***6132,*** 1997
6" x 3" x 9" (15 x 7.5 x 23 cm). White stoneware; thrown, trimmed, hand-built, altered, and assembled; glazed; reduction fired to cone 10; sandblasted

Top right: **Ruth Duckworth,** ***Untitled,*** 1997
28½" x 16" x 6" (72.5 x 40.5 x 15 cm). Porcelain; glazed; high fire in gas reduction. Photo by James Prinz

Left: **Aase Haũgaard,** ***Jar from the Subsoil,*** 1997
16½" x 11¾" x 11¾" (42 x 30 x 30 cm). Thrown, surface structure created with a tool, top coiled and added; sprayed copper carbonate and slips; bisque fired; raku glazed top; saggar fired with sawdust and vermiculite to 1300°C (2372°F)

Top left: **Ted Randall (1914-1985),** ***Light Box,*** 1982
Height: 15½" (39.5 cm). Stoneware.
Photo courtesy of Tom Randall

Top right: **Peg Malloy,** ***Oval Box,*** 1996
6½" x 8½" x 4½" (16.5 x 21.5 x 11.5 cm). Porcelain; thrown without a bottom, shaped into an oval, and attached to slab bottom; lid thrown in two pieces; shino slip applied to bone-dry ware; fired in a Bourry box kiln to cone 10-11. Photo by artist

Right: **Peter Voulkos,** ***Nemo,*** 1997
43½" x 24" x 24" (110.5 x 61 x 61 cm). Stoneware; thrown, altered, and stacked; wood fired. Peter Voulkos is known as the originator of abstract impression in modern claywork. Photo courtesy of Perimeter Gallery, Chicago, IL

Left: **Michael J. Knox II,** ***Untitled,*** 1997
37" x 11" x 7½" (94 x 28 x 19 cm). Stoneware; thrown vessels, slab-built shelves; bisque fired; glazed; each unit fired to cone 10 with vessel in the hanging position. Photo by artist

Below: **Mark Messenger,** ***Biomorphic Pyre,*** 1996
20" x 10" x 9" (51 x 25.5 x 23 cm). Earthenware; pieces thrown, paddled, and altered when leather hard; clay added and removed to create relief, sculpted elements connected in stack, original elements carved and sculpted, lid fit; underglazes and glazes; oxidation fired to cone 06. Photo by Ken Von Schlegel

Top left: **Anonymous,** ***Vase,*** Chinese adaptation, Jugtown Pottery, Moore County, NC, made prior to 1953
Height: 8" (20.5 cm). Jugtown Pottery was established in 1917 by Jaques and Juliana Busbee in order to revive the traditional pottery of the area; they employed local potters. The Busbees also introduced the Jugtown potters to Chinese and Korean forms and glazes. Photo courtesy of Sid Oakley and the Museum of American Pottery

Bottom left: **Makoto Hatori,** ***Bizen Facet "Youhen" Water Pot,*** 1997
7½" x 7¼" x 7¼" (19 x 18.5 x 18.5 cm). Bizen stoneware; thrown and faceted by trimming with a knife when leather hard; wood reduction fired in Japanese bank kiln for ten days to 1300°C (2372°F); natural wood-ash glaze ("youhen" means "fire change"). Photo by artist

Top right: **Warren MacKenzie,** ***Pentagonal Box,*** 1996
7" x 7¾" x 7¾" (18 x 19.5 x 19.5 cm). Stoneware; thrown, stretched, then beaten; Surformed surface; reduction fired in gas kiln to cone 11. Photo by Peter Lee.

Bottom right: **Kevin A. Myers,** ***Untitled,*** 1997
8" x 8" x 7½" (20.5 x 20.5 x 19 cm). Low-fire clay; thrown, cut, incised, pushed out, torn; slip-trailed dots, spikes applied; sprayed red glaze, transparent glaze on window; fired to cone 06; gold luster; luster fired to cone 018. Photo by Anthony Cuñha

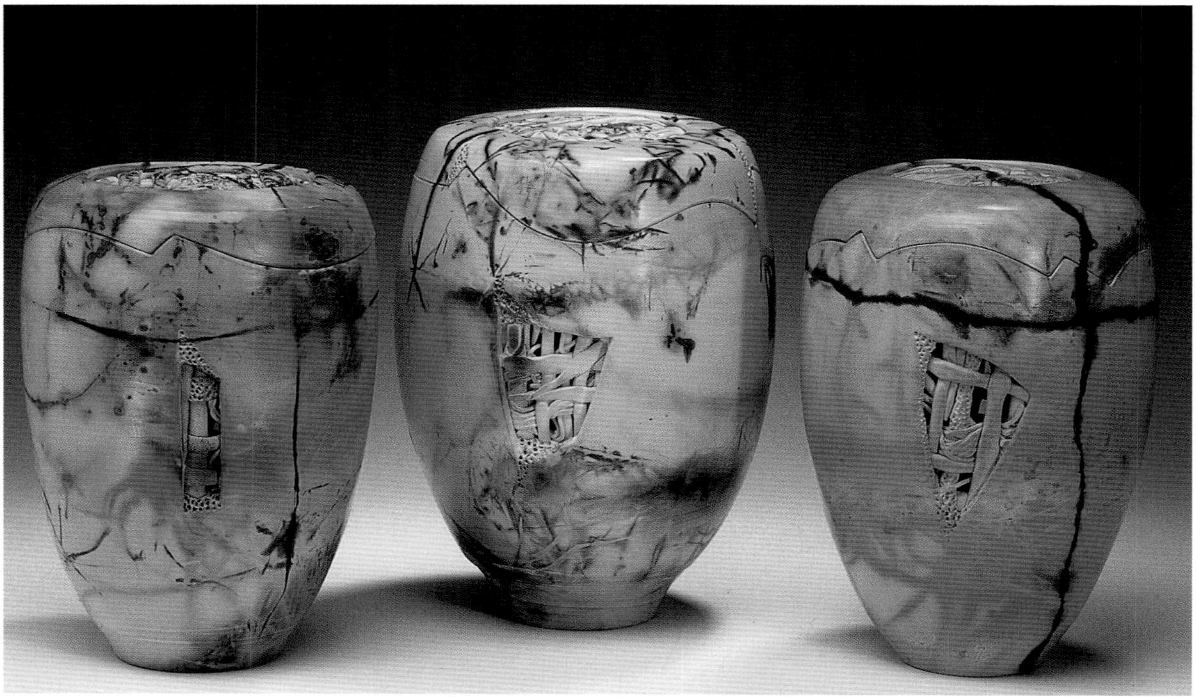

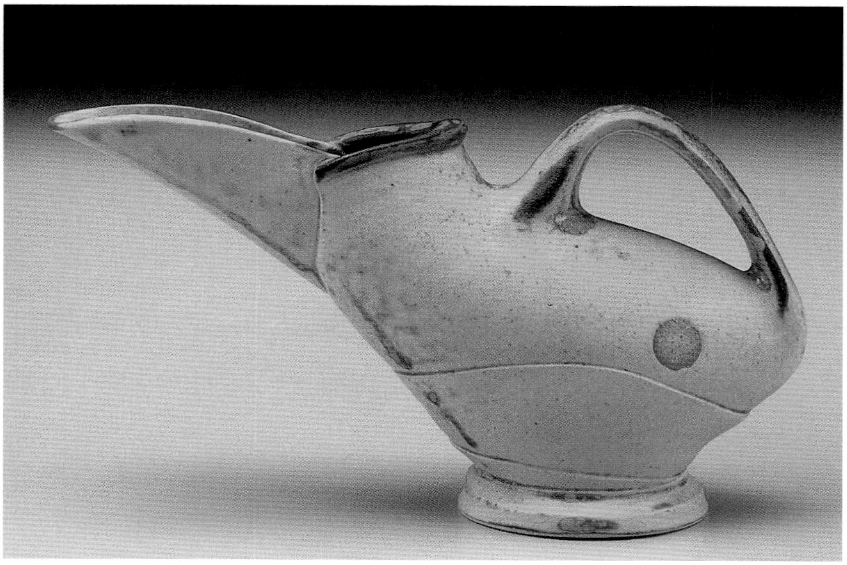

Top: **Judith E. Motzkin,** ***Trio of Boxes with Woven Windows,*** 1997
Height of tallest: 12" (30.5 cm). Earthenware; thrown, cut when leather hard, woven coil inlay added to top opening and cut-open windows in side walls; polished terra sigillata; saggar fired in gas kiln to cone 06. Photo by Bob Barrett

Bottom left: **Kouji Sugie,** ***Bottle,*** 1995
7¼" x 3½" x 3¾" (18.5 x 9 x 9.5 cm). Local Tokoname clay; thrown; wood-fired on its side for five days (some bamboo used as fuel during firing). Photo by Dick Lehman

Bottom right: **Nicholas Joerling,** ***Pitcher (small),*** 1997
4" x 2½" x 6" (10 x 6.5 x 15 cm). Stoneware; thrown, made oval, cut, and reassembled; slab spout and handle added; shino glaze, brushed wax resist, reglazed; reduction fired in gas kiln to cone 10. Photo by Tim Barnwell

CHAPTER FOUR

Wheel-Thrown and Altered Projects

Neil Patterson, *Bottle Form,* 1997
8" x 6" x 5" (20.5 x 15 x 12.5 cm). White stoneware; thrown and textured components, cut apart and assembled into new shapes; slip applied; wood fired to cone 11, light salt glaze. Photo by artist

Wheel-Thrown and Altered Projects

The projects in this chapter are presented in a sequence. The first is a cylindrical spoon vase. This project is a variation on the basic cylindrical form and also introduces a couple of simple altering techniques—the techniques by which a form is changed after throwing. The next two basic forms covered are the bowl and the plate. By the time you're comfortable with these forms, you'll have mastered the basics of throwing.

During the learning process, you'll find it helpful to make these pieces as they're shown and in the order they're presented. Most students go through a phase when their work looks very much like the instructor's examples. This phase will pass as you achieve technical facility, and when you do, your own style will become more evident. When you reach the point at which throwing is no longer a technical struggle, the forms that you make can begin to flow. You, the clay, and the wheel will develop a sense of harmony, and you'll be ready to begin intentionally exploring forms.

With the pitcher, wavy oval vase, and teapot projects, you'll be entering an "advanced" section, so work up to these forms gradually. The heart-shaped vase and torso vase variation, in which techniques for making larger forms are introduced, are also presented for skilled potters, who I hope will adapt these projects to their own purposes. I offer them in the spirit that we're all students, with ever more to learn.

Interspersed among the projects are a wide range of variations that I've developed myself, as well as a number of projects developed and demonstrated by fellow potters who very generously agreed to share their techniques.

Most potters explore and develop thrown forms by working in series—throwing a group of similar forms. In my studio, for example, I'll spend a day throwing bowls. The next day, I'll alter and shape them, and the day after that, I'll trim them and prepare for the next day's venture.

Repetition is essential in order to become truly familiar with a form. Many potters develop a repertoire of shapes that they continue to investigate and develop for many years. The cycle of throwing, glazing, and firing provides its own natural breaks as you make these shapes. Exhibiting or selling your work, if you're at that stage of development as a potter, will provide yet another break (sometimes a major distraction) in the cycle.

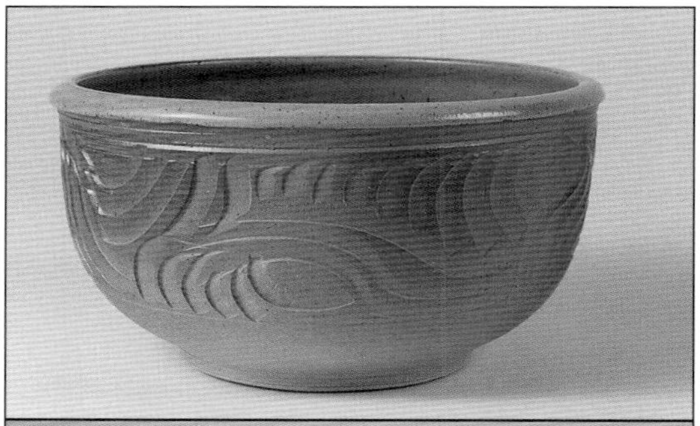

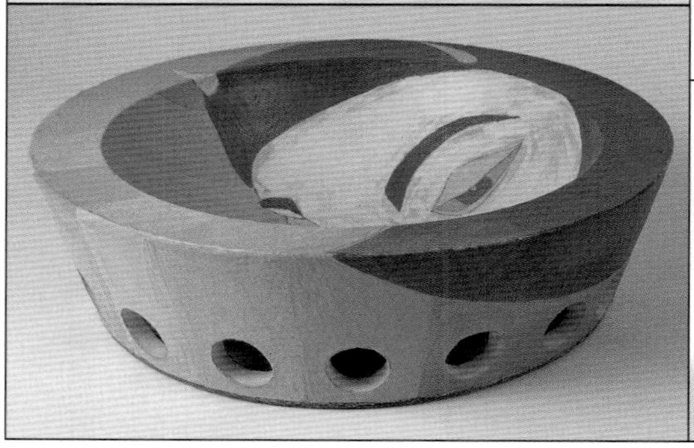

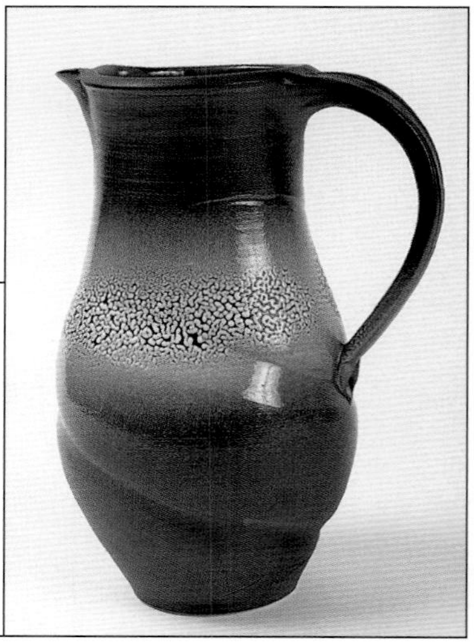

Starting Tips

- Before you begin, make sure you have a basic set of potter's tools (see page 8). Then read the instructions for the project you'd like to make. You'll find that any other required tools are mentioned in these instructions.

- Unless the instructions tell you otherwise, you can assume that any turning wheel shown in a project photo is turning in a counterclockwise direction.

- When I made these projects, I used a white porcelaneous clay. If you're just beginning to throw, you'll be more successful with a stoneware clay that has a little more tooth.

- The project instructions don't cover surface treatments in any detail, but a wide range of treatments and applications are described in chapter 5.

- Remember that the more the inner and outer contours of a thrown piece reflect each other, the better balanced the piece will be.

- No matter what project you're throwing, stabilize your hands by bracing them against each other whenever possible.

After throwing steadily for a couple of weeks, it's sometimes several more weeks before I have time to return to the wheel. By then, as the pieces I last threw have moved through the cycle, I've thoroughly examined them. Ideas for developing these forms occur at every stage of the cycle, and when I'm back at the wheel again, I approach the same forms in a new light. I never cease to be amazed by the ways in which even the most subtle variations can change the feeling that a form projects.

If you're interested in making sculpture, all of the forming methods demonstrated in these projects are directly applicable to creating purely sculptural work. All thrown forms are variations of the cone, cylinder, or sphere—the basic elements of three-dimensional design. These forms may also be paddled and pushed to become pyramids, rectangles, or squares.

Even though the projects in this chapter are functional pots, they deal with considerations of form and content quite similar to those of sculpture. Pieces thrown on the potter's wheel can be ideal beginnings for figurative, abstract, and nonrepresentational expressions.

Spoon Vase

A simple cylindrical form is a good one with which to begin your first forays into altering. The cylinder itself is relatively easy to throw, and you won't be making any big investments in materials or time, either. The cylindrical spoon-vase project presented here demonstrates throwing a wide lip and altering it, and altering the surface of the form to create an indented spiral pattern.

The effects of altering a thrown form can range from vigorous and gutsy to gracefully elegant. To the student who is striving to master the skill of throwing, altering will probably seem a bit absurd. Why throw a perfectly symmetrical form and then mess it up? This is a reasonable question. Many beautiful and soulful pots are thrown without any altering beyond the initial throwing process.

After I'd refined my own throwing skills, I started to feel that some of my work looked too perfect and too stiff after firing. It had lost the sensual feeling of the clay. When I developed and used the altering techniques shown in some of these projects, my finished pieces started to reflect more of the soft feeling that I love in wet, pliable clay.

This spoon vase requires 2 pounds (.9 kg) of clay. (Just vary the amount for larger or smaller vessels.) Throwing it is almost exactly like throwing the cylinder described on pages 34-43, so you may want to review those instructions before beginning.

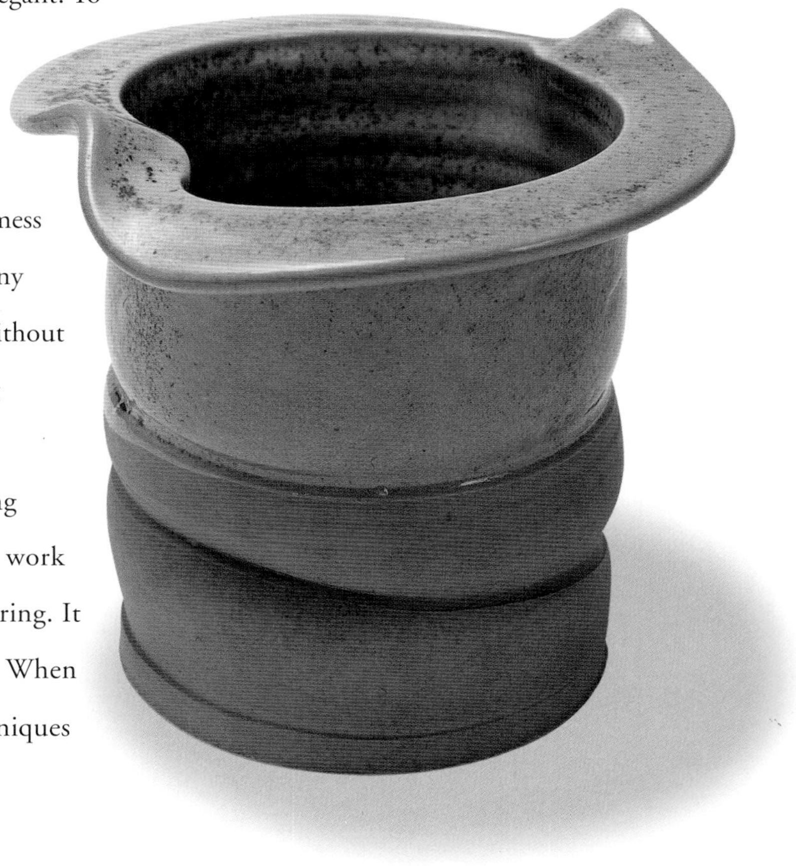

Surface Treatment and Firing

Bisque fired to cone 06
Interior and upper portion of exterior glazed
Exterior glaze etched through with large nail
Lower portion sprayed with iron-oxide solution
Glaze fired to cone 9, light reduction in gas-fired kiln

Instructions

1. After preparing your clay, center it on the bat or wheel head and open it just as you would if you were making a flat-bottomed cylinder.
2. On your first pull, leave extra clay at the rim as you reach the top. You'll need enough clay in that area to form the exaggerated lip.

3. At the top of the next pull, pull this extra clay outward, shaping it as desired (Photos 1 and 2). Working on a rim like this one requires a delicate touch and a very slow wheel speed.

1

2

4. Make the third pull. You're likely to do more smoothing and shaping than actual pulling at this stage.

5. To remove the marks left by your fingers during pulling, hold a flexible metal rib against the outside of the clay wall, and as the wheel turns at your pulling speed, push the rib inward while the fingers of your left hand support the wall from the inside. Be sure to hold the rib at the correct angle, with the edge that contacts the clay farthest from you. The rib should smooth the clay, not dig into it (Photo 3).

3

6. To create the indented spiral effect, first set a comfortably slow wheel speed. Then, starting at the bottom of the cylinder and holding the rib at an angle, push the tip of the rib into the clay and, using Photo 4 as a guide, move it straight upward as far as you like. I stop the rib just past the center of the cylinder.

4

7. As soon as you've indented the spoon vase, you'll alter the rim. To do this, stop the wheel and hold the rim with the thumb and forefinger of each hand. Then move one hand up and the other down (Photo 5). Be careful to do this delicately; the clay will stretch only to a given point before tearing. (The rim is also likely to tear if it's too thin.) Repeat to alter the opposite side of the rim.

8. Separate the piece from the bat if necessary and remove it immediately after altering. Allow it to dry uncovered until it is leather hard. Finish the bottom by rolling it on a table top to bevel the sharp bottom edge and then running your finger around the edge to remove any sharpness.

Variations

To create variations in the indented spiral pattern, reduce or increase the pressure you apply with the rib, move the rib upward at a different speed, or waver it up and down a bit as it moves upward. Using different tools will also create different line qualities.

For a different effect at the rim, try varying its thickness and angle, or use your fingers to shape it as desired.

After letting the spoon vase stiffen a bit, use your hands to change its shape.

As you can see in the photo of the mugs shown below, even a basic cylindrical form can be subtly shaped. For instructions on shaping, refer to the pitcher project on pages 82-88.

Possible Problems and Solutions

Problem: The body of the pot bends out of shape as you pull the rim.

Solution: You may be pulling out too quickly. If the body hasn't twisted too much, try straightening it by pushing lightly against the outside with a rib while supporting the clay on the inside with your fingers. If this doesn't work, throw another cylinder and try pulling out the rim more gradually so that you move less clay at a time. The body may also twist out of shape if one area of the wall is too thin or too soft. Pull another piece if this happens.

Problem: The rib snags as you attempt to create the spiral denting.

Solution: Try decreasing the angle between the rib and the clay.

Problem: When you're altering the rim, the clay seems too soft to hold its shape.

Solution: Set the pot aside, uncovered, until the clay has stiffened a bit. Then try again.

Right: **George Ohr**, ***Vessel,*** circa 1900
7½" x 7½" x 7½" (19 x 19 x 19 cm). Earthenware. George Ohr was a pioneer in altering thrown forms; his work inspires many contemporary potters. Photo courtesy of Garth Clark Gallery, New York, NY

Far right: **Richey Bellinger,** ***Squared Vase #2,*** 1997
14" x 6" x 6" (35.5 x 15 x 15 cm). Porcelain; bottomless cylinder thrown, slip decoration added and tooled with rib with wheel turning slowly, squared from inside, bottom thrown and attached at leather-hard stage, lug handles added; bisque fired; sprayed slip glazes; reduction fired to cone 10. Photo by artist

Bottom left: **Tim Turner,** ***Vessel,*** 1997
10" x 8" x 6" (25.5 x 20.5 x 15 cm). Stoneware; thrown, altered, slab bottom added when body leather hard; dipped in thin copper slip and salt glazed; wood fired to cone 10

Bottom right: **Dick Lehman,** ***Squared Sidefired Jar,*** 1996
7½" x 5½" x 5½" (19 x 14 x 14 cm). Porcelain; thrown, altered by stretching out four corners; handles rolled, textured, twisted, and attached while pot wet; carbon-trapping glaze applied; wood ashes, fluxes, and colorants sprinkled on while glaze still wet; reduction fired in gas kiln to cone 10, on tripod, with glazed side facing up; ashes, fluxes, and colorants run to bottom to create "front" of piece. Photo by artist

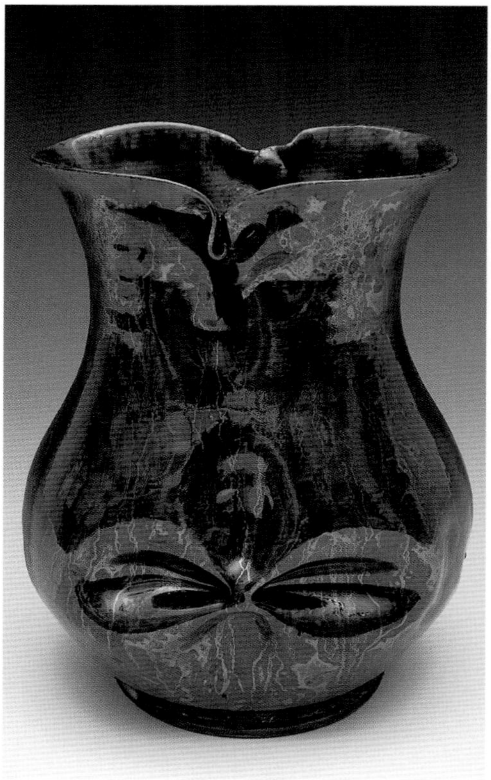

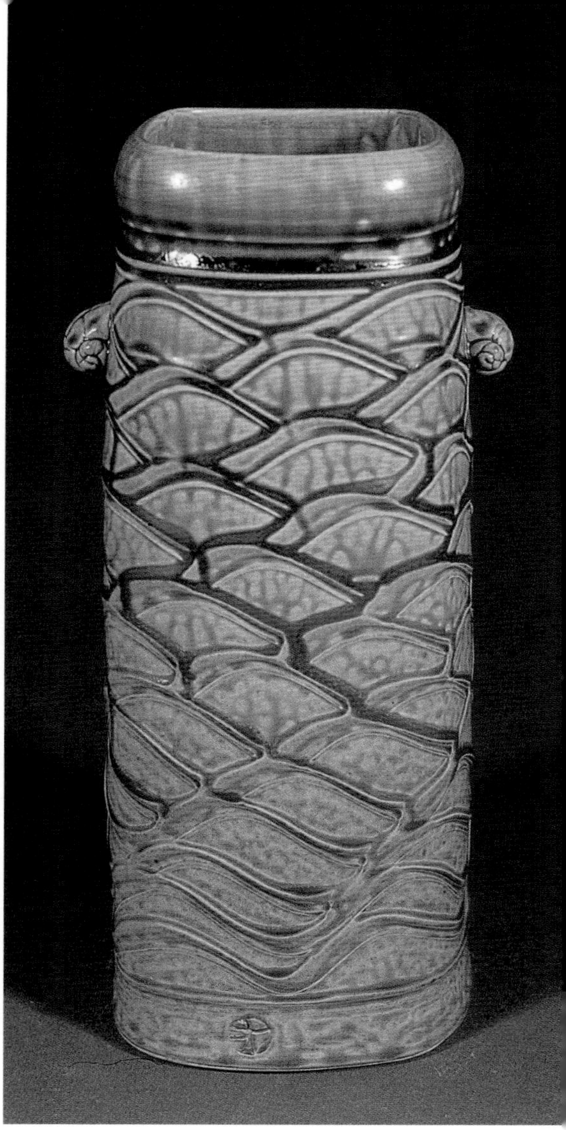

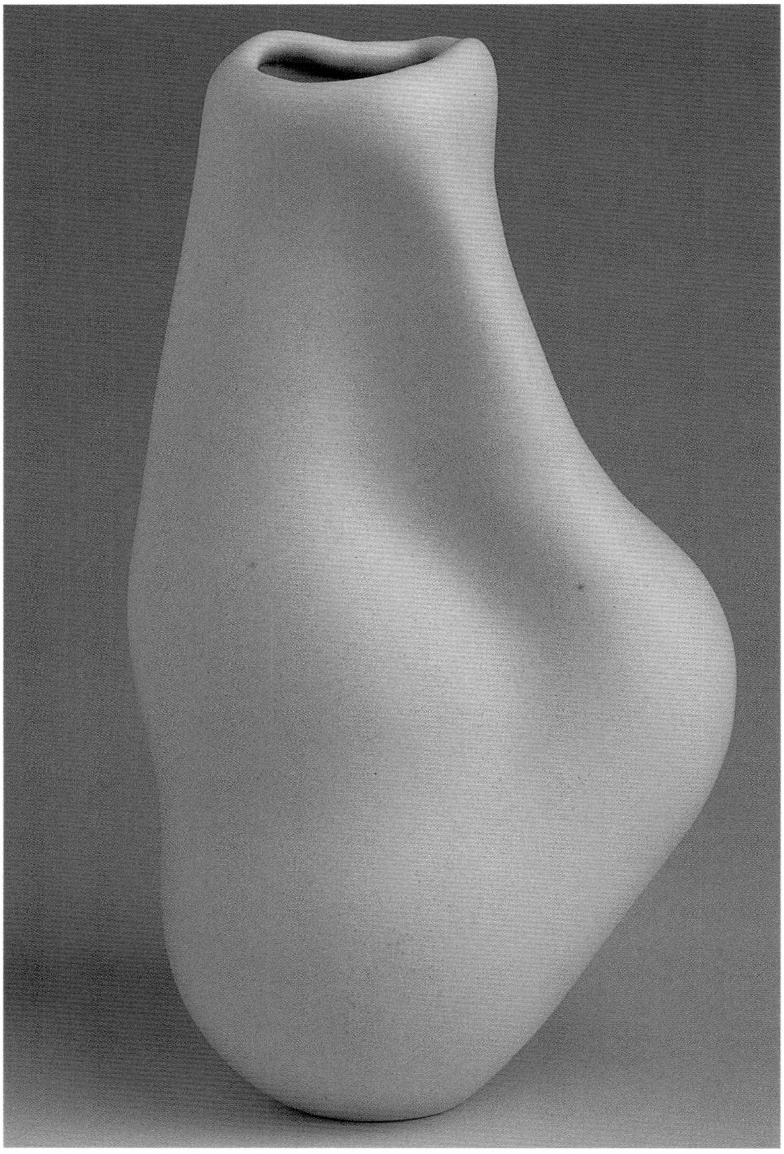

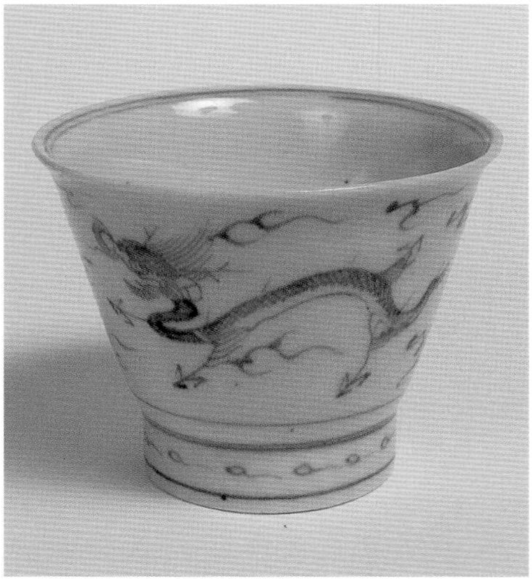

Top left: **Rick Urban,** ***Untitled,*** 1996
Height: 4" (10 cm). Porcelain; thrown, with altered rim; salt glazed; fired to cone 10. Photo by Tim Barnwell

Top right: **Malcolm Davis,** ***Shino Tea Bowl,*** 1995
3½" x 3" x 3" (9 x 7.5 x 7.5 cm). Porcelain; thrown and squared; shino-type carbon trap glaze; reduction fired to cone 10 (very heavy body reduction at cone 012)

Center right: ***Japanese Imari Soba Cup,*** 18th century
3" x 3½" x 3½" (7.5 x 9 x 9 cm). Porcelain, underglaze cobalt blue brushwork; protected by a saggar from ash during wood firing. Sets of these small cups were made for serving soba noodles. The exquisite brushwork on this piece is rarely matched. Collection of Don Davis; photo by Evan Bracken

Left: **Lola J. Logsdon,** ***Untitled,*** 1991
11½" x 6" x 5" (29 x 15 x 12.5 cm). White stoneware; thrown and altered cylinder; multiple glazes; multiple firings in electric kiln to cone 5 and cone 04. Photo by John Buffington Photographic Services, Colorado State University

Right: **Chris Staley,** ***4 Stoneware Cups,*** 1996
10" x 12" x 4" (25.5 x 30.5 x 10 cm). Stoneware; thrown, with pulled handles; wax resist, dipped slips; light salt firing to cone 9

Below: **Sam Clarkson,** ***Celadon Teaset,*** 1997
12" x 12" x 20" (30.5 x 30.5 x 51 cm). Porcelain; pots thrown, wire-cut, expanded from inside; platter walls thrown, wire-cut, and added to slab; pots heavy reduction fired to cone 9; platter wood fired. Photo by Tracy Hicks

Bowl

This project introduces several techniques, including a variation on centering and on the first pull, trimming a foot ring, flaring a rim, and trimming an altered bowl.

As with any form, it's best to start small and work your way up to larger sizes. The medium-sized serving bowl presented here requires 5 pounds (2.3 kg) of clay. Use 1½ to 2 pounds (.7 to .9 kg) for a soup, salad, or dessert-sized bowl and 7 to 10 pounds (3.2 to 4.5 kg) for a large bowl.

The shape of this bowl is inspired by the classic shape of a Chinese Song Dynasty bowl. Its vertical foot gives it some "lift" from the surface upon which it sits, and the difference between the diameters of the foot and the rim creates visual tension without being so extreme as to make the bowl look unstable. The slight curve of the wall, as the eye follows it from bottom to top, also adds some excitement to the form.

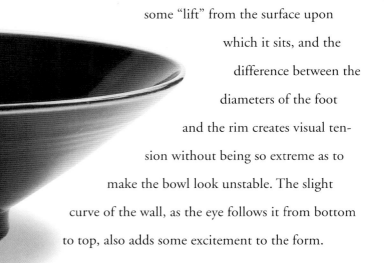

Surface Treatment and Firing

Bisque fired to cone 06

Interior and exterior glazed

Glaze fired to cone 9, light reduction in gas-fired kiln

Instructions

1. Prepare the clay by wedging it well. Pat it into a ball or cone shape and place it on the bat. As the wheel turns very slowly, push the clay on both sides a few times to help move it to the center.
2. With this technique, you'll start shaping the clay from the very beginning. Even the way you center it will lead toward the bowl shape. Using Photo 1 as a guide, center the clay to form a large door-

1

knob shape by applying pressure at the base to narrow it. The wheel should be turning at the fastest speed that's comfortable for you.

3. Slow the wheel down a little from its centering speed in preparation for opening. The finished bowl will have a trimmed foot (see steps 9 to 14), so as you open the clay, leave the bottom at least twice as thick as you would on a flat-bottomed piece. You'll trim away a portion of this thick bottom to create the foot ring. The required thickness will vary, of course, depending on how tall you want the foot to be. On this piece, the bottom is approximately ¾ inch (1.9 cm) thick.

4. Slow down the wheel to pulling speed. Then make the first pull by using the thumb and fingers of your left hand to pull the clay upward and outward, while your right hand serves as a guide to contain the rim (Photo 2). (If you like, you may use this pulling technique for first pulls on other forms, including cylinders.)

2

5. To make subsequent pulls, switch to the technique described on pages 38-40, using the middle finger of each hand to move the clay upward and outward (Photo 3). Your last pull should serve to finalize and make the shape even, rather than moving the clay any farther upward or outward (Photo 4).

6. You may need to slow down the wheel again before taking this step. Working from the bottom of the bowl up to its top, smooth and shape the interior surface by using your left hand to hold a curved wooden rib against the clay on the inside and supporting the clay from the outside with your right hand (Photo 5).

3

4

5

7. Working from bottom to top again, smooth and shape the exterior surface by using your right hand to hold the flat edge of a flexible metal rib against the outer wall, while supporting the clay on the inside with your left hand (Photo 6). You'll need to bend the rib in your hand to form a slight curve. To finalize the form, repeat this alternate ribbing several times on the interior and exterior surfaces.

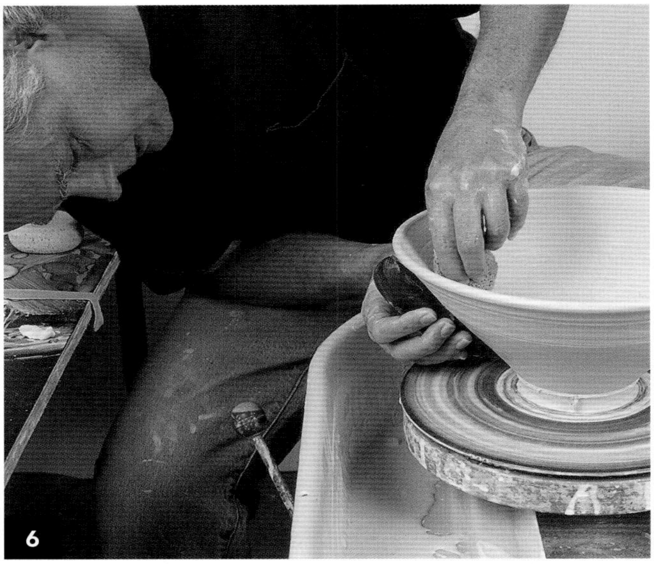

6

8. If you're throwing on a nonabsorbent bat, separate the bowl from the bat with your wire, but leave the bowl in place in order to avoid distorting it. Set the bat and bowl aside and allow the bowl to dry to leather hard. As it stiffens, be sure to rotate it every hour or so; this will prevent moving air from drying one side more quickly than the other. You may need to cover the rim with plastic, as it will always dry faster than the bottom. If the rim dries too much before you turn the leather-hard bowl upside down for trimming, it's likely to crack when you turn it over. (Dry clay loses its flexibility.)

9. When the bowl is leather hard, turn it upside down onto a bat in preparation for trimming the foot. The trimming bat shown in Photo 7 has a soft, rubbery coating on its surface and is an ideal tool for bowl and plate trimming because it won't mar the rim of a leather-hard clay form and because it holds the piece in place by "grabbing" it. An alternative is to place the bowl on a plaster or plastic bat and hold it in place with four wads of moist clay, positioned in opposing pairs around its rim (Photo 8). Push the wads down onto the bat, not inward.

7

8

10. Your trimming won't succeed unless the bowl is centered. If your bat has concentric circles on it, use them as guides when you position the bowl. (You can use a pencil to draw your own concentric rings on any bat or wheel head. Just hold the pencil against the bat and let the wheel turn.) Then, with the wheel turning at the speed that's most comfortable for you, center the bowl by using your right hand to tap it repeatedly. This may seem to be a tricky process at first, but once mastered, it's a valuable skill. An alternative to tapping is to start and stop the wheel, readjusting the bowl's position each time. If uneven drying has caused the rim to warp at all, remember that the portion you're centering is the part you plan to trim—in this case, the foot.

11. Using a loop trimming tool, establish the outer diameter of the foot first, trimming it down to a dimension just slightly larger than the desired final diameter (Photo 7). You can always remove more clay later, but once you've trimmed it away, it's gone! When your clay is at just the right stage of leather hard, it will come off easily in curled, ribbonlike strips. Clay that's too soft will be sticky, and clay that's too hard will chip and will be difficult to trim.

12. Using Photo 9 as a guide, trim away the inner portion of the foot. Use the narrow end of a pear-shaped trimming tool to do this, moving it back

9

and forth across the clay, starting from what will be the inner edge of the foot ring. Keep in mind that you'll need to trim deeper at the inner edge of the ring than in the center of the bottom in order to reflect the curved interior contour of the bowl. You'll need to make several passes to remove enough clay. The thickness of the bottom you established when you opened the clay will determine how deep you can go as you trim.

13. I use a small trimming tool to complete the trimming and to establish the final thickness and height of the foot ring. I also round off the foot ring instead of leaving it flat (Photo 10). If you intend to glaze the interior of the foot ring, it must be deep enough to ensure that the glaze on the bottom of the bowl won't touch the kiln shelf when the bowl is fired.

10

14. To compress and burnish the trimmed areas, use a rib on the outer surface of the foot ring and the rounded end of a wooden stick on the inner area surrounded by the foot ring (Photo 11). This bowl and the variations described in the next section may be left uncovered to dry after trimming.

11

Variations

One way to alter a classic bowl is to flare the rim before trimming the foot. (The bowls shown in the photo above were altered in this fashion.) Right after throwing, with the wheel turning slowly, carefully press the flat edge of a wooden stick down onto the moist clay (Photo 12). As you do this, position the other hand underneath the clay rim to support it. The flattened rim must be left angled slightly upward, or it will collapse. Now cut the bowl free from the bat and leave it in place on the bat to stiffen.

12

Flared rims often move back up as they dry. When I make a flared bowl, I let it stiffen for an hour or so, uncovered, on the bat. Then I center it again on the wheel and, with the wheel turning slowly, push the rim back down with a flat stick. If you let the piece dry too long, the rim will split as you do this, so monitor the drying form carefully. Also remember to rotate it every 15 minutes or so to avoid uneven drying.

To finish this flared bowl, immediately after adjusting the rim and before the foot is trimmed, I apply an engobe with a flat brush, turning the wheel while holding the brush in position (Photo 13). The rim must be almost stiff enough for foot trimming at this stage, or it may collapse under the pressure of the brush. To create a crisp, lively design, I then stop the wheel and comb a toothed rib through the engobe (Photo 14). Once the engobe has dried to leather hard, the bowl can be turned upside down and trimmed.

13

14

Another way to alter a classic bowl shape is to create an oval form by gently pressing in the sides of the piece when it's at the soft leather-hard stage (see the photo above). Trimming an altered form such as an oval bowl can be a special challenge. In this case, because the bowl will no longer sit evenly on its rim, you'll need to hold it in a cylindrical chuck. To make the chuck, throw a cylinder narrow enough to fit up into the inside bottom of the altered bowl. (You may use this chuck when it's leather hard, dry, or bisqued.) Cover the open end of the chuck with a folded towel or some thin foam rubber so that it won't mar the interior of the leather-hard bowl (Photo 15). Then center the chuck on the wheel.

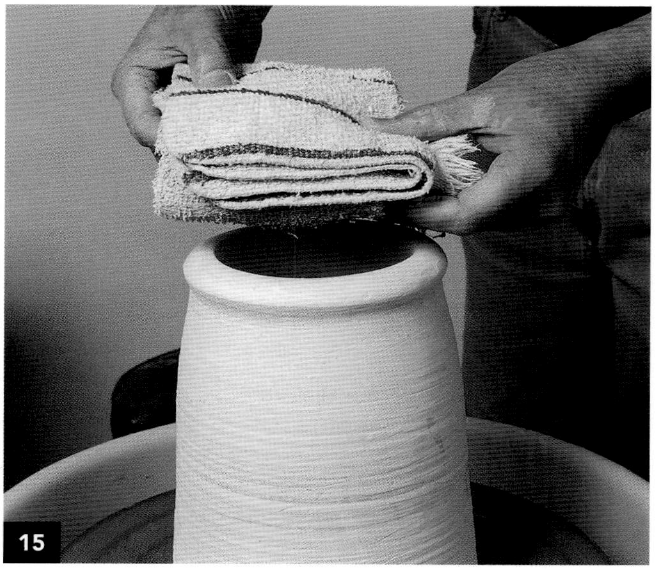

15

Turn the altered bowl upside down and place it on top of the padded chuck, adjusting it until the bottom is centered. (Only the bottom of this piece can be trimmed on the wheel, as the bottom is the only portion you can center.) On this bowl, after trimming the foot ring, I cut openings through the ring to alter its appearance (Photo 16). Then I smooth the rough edges of the foot with a small, damp sponge. To complete the final shaping of the body and blend it with the trimmed area, I smooth it with a small, flexible metal rib and my fingers.

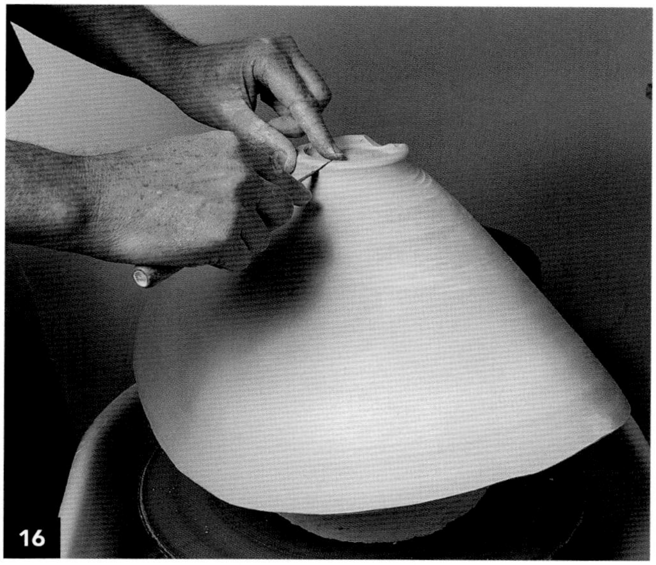

16

Possible Problems and Solutions

Problem: The bowl becomes soft and wobbly as you're shaping it on the wheel.

Solution: Leave it on the bat, remove the bat from wheel, and let the bowl stiffen until it's ready to take on the shaping. To avoid uneven drying or overdrying, remember to rotate the bowl periodically and monitor it carefully. You may need to cover the rim lightly with plastic to keep it from drying faster than the bottom.

Problem: The rim dries to the point of inflexibility before you trim the bottom.

Solution: Make sure you pad the surface that the rim will sit on as you trim. Next time, cover the rim with plastic before it becomes too dry and let the bottom catch up. Alternatively, turn the bowl upside down as soon as the rim firms up enough to hold the weight of the pot. This will expose the bottom of the bowl to more air and will help it catch up with the rim.

Top left: **Don Davis, *Tripod Bowl,*** 1997
Height: 5" (12.5 cm). Porcelain; thrown, with wavy rim and added feet; bisque fired to cone 06; interior glazed, tape resist and oxide spray on exterior; glaze fired to cone 7, light reduction. Photo by Evan Bracken

Above: **Katharine Gotham, *Bowling League,*** 1996
Each: 3½" x 5½" x 4½" (9 x 14 x 11.5 cm). Stoneware with iron; thrown and altered with palms of hands; wax resist design, latex resist used between color dips; soda fired to cone 9. Photo by John Lehn Studio

Left: **Chris Simoncelli, *Porcelain Bowl,*** 1996
4½" x 15½" x 15½" (11.5 x 39.5 x 39.5 cm). Thrown; painted glazes; fired in electric kiln to cone 6. Photo by artist

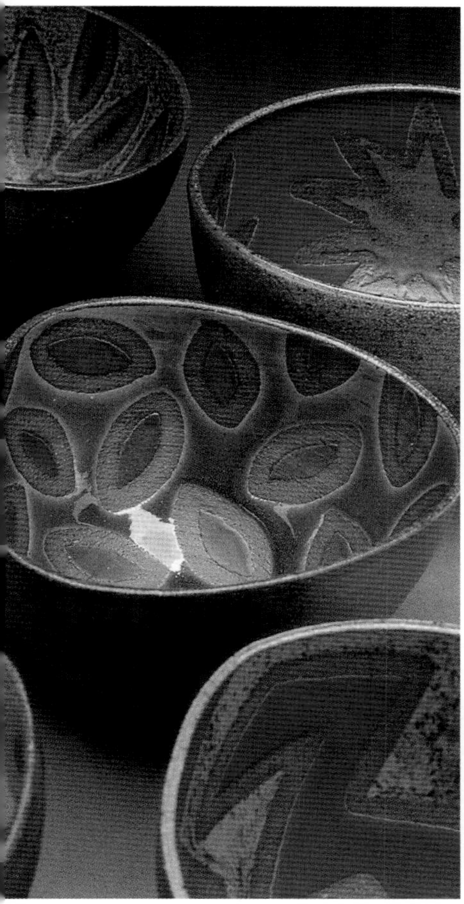

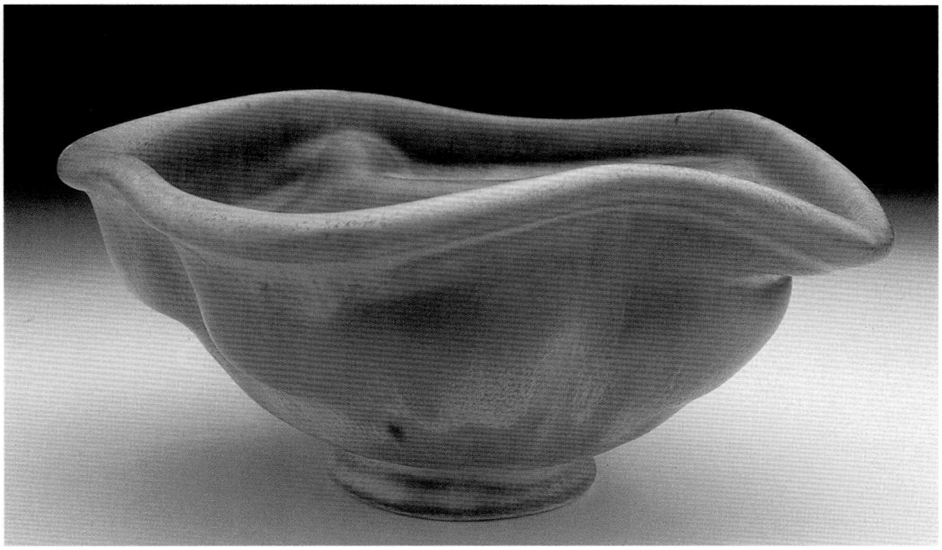

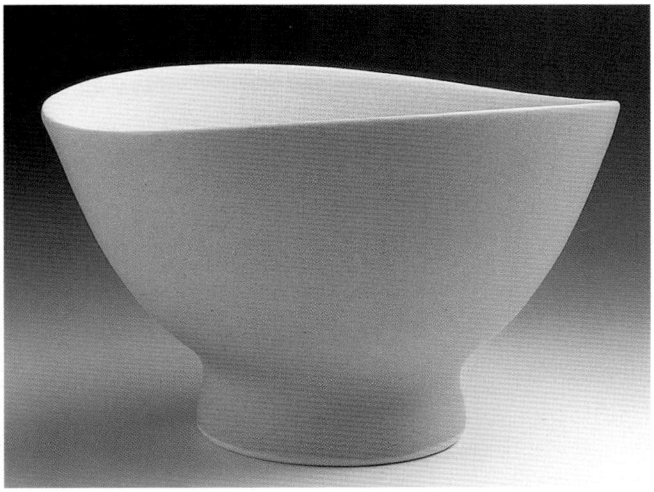

Top right: **Harriet E. Ross, *Baking Dish,*** 1997
4½" x 10" x 5½" (11.5 x 25.5 x 14 cm). Stoneware; thrown and altered body; feet thrown, cut, and added; handles added; dipped and brushed glaze; reduction fired in gas kiln to cone 10.
Photo by artist

Center right: **Shannon Nelson, *Bowl About Softness,*** 1997
3" x 6½" x 6" (7.5 x 16.5 x 15 cm). Porcelaneous stoneware; thrown and altered by hand, foot trimmed; glazed; reduction fired to cone 10. Photo by artist

Bottom right: **Neville French, *Porcelain Bowl,*** 1995
5½" x 7" x 6¼" (14 x 18 x 16 cm). Thrown, cradled and slowly scraped, pressed at various drying stages; multiple layers of sprayed glazes; oxidation fired in gas kiln to cone 10. Photo by Terence Bogue

Top: **Cynthia Bringle,** ***Colander,*** 1997
4" x 12" (10 x 30.5 cm). Stoneware; thrown and altered when wet, holes punched at leather-hard stage; wood and salt fired to cone 10.
Photo by Tim Barnwell

Center: **Don Davis,** ***Tripod Dish,*** 1997
Diameter: 12" (30.5 cm). Porcelain; thrown, with wavy rim and added feet; engobe with paper resist pattern on interior; bisque fired to cone 06; interior glazed, iron oxide solution sprayed on rim and exterior; glaze fired to cone 7, light reduction.
Photo by Tim Barnwell

Left: **Michael E. Rutkowsky,** ***Casserole,*** 1997
8" x 9" x 9" (20.5 x 23 x 23 cm). Stoneware; thrown base and lid, knob thrown on lid; brushed slip glazes and trailed glazes, with finger-combed beige slip; reduction fired in gas kiln to cone 10.
Photo by Tom Mills

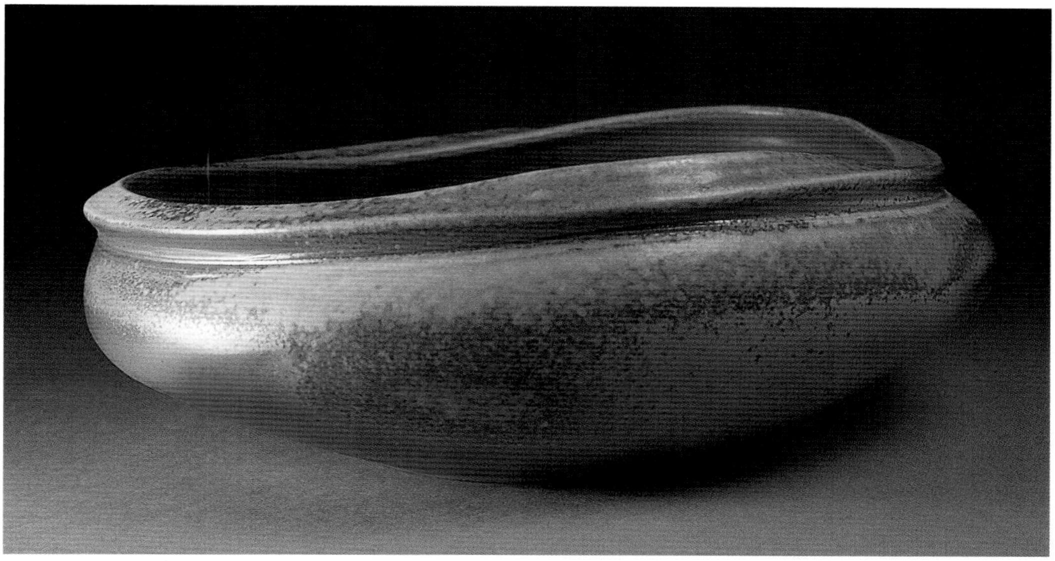

Top right: **Peg Malloy, *Altered Bowl,*** 1997
12" x 12½" x 5" (30.5 x 32 x 12.5 cm). Porcelain; thrown, rim stiffened with heat gun and wall pushed out with rubber rib; shino slip applied to bone-dry ware; wood fired in a Bourry box kiln to cone 10-11. Photo by artist

Above: **Hans Coper, *Composite Form,*** circa 1967
Height: 7½" (19 cm). Stoneware. Coper was an innovator in the use of thrown vessels as the basis for purely sculptural forms. Private collection. Photo courtesy of Garth Clark Gallery, New York, NY

Right: **Keiko Fukazawa, *Gift from the Sea I,*** 1996
10" x 8" x 9" (25.5 x 20.5 x 23 cm). White earthenware; stack-thrown bowl with turned bottom; bowl inverted to create dripping slip effect, then joined to hand-built base; textured with rock, slip-cast shapes; bisque fired to cone 08; oxidation glaze fired to cone 06. Photo by Anthony Cuñha

CARVED BOWL

Cynthia Bringle uses a loop trimming tool to carve this bowl in a free-flowing, nonrepetitive design; her designs are completely spontaneous. The outer surfaces of carved pots such as this one can be glazed or left unglazed. Alternatives include rubbing a stain or oxide solution into the carved areas, or dipping the exterior in a glaze that will cover the design without obliterating it. Many glazes will accentuate carved textures and create pleasing effects over and around the edges of the carved areas.

This bowl is made with 7 pounds (3.2 kg) of stoneware clay.

Surface Treatment and Firing

Interior glazed

Wood and salt fired

Instructions

1. Prepare the clay by wedging it well. Pat it into a ball and place it on the bat. As the wheel turns very slowly, push the clay on both sides a few times to help move it to the center.
2. Because this piece of clay is too large to fit between your cupped hands, you'll have to center it in a slightly different fashion from the one described on pages 34-36. First, make sure your hands and the clay are moist. Then, with the wheel rotating at your centering speed, press the large lump of clay firmly between your cupped hands to form a relatively tall cone (Photo 1). This process is known as "coning up." Then push the clay back down to center it on the wheel.

3. Pull the bowl and shape it, making sure to leave the wall thick enough to allow you to carve the outer surface. After completing the final shaping, use a rib to smooth the interior and exterior surfaces (Photo 2).

2

4. Cynthia uses her fingernail to etch a line just below the rim of her bowl (Photo 3). This line will serve as the upper border of the carved area.

3

5. Cut the bowl free from the bat, if necessary, and set it aside to stiffen to medium leather hard. Be sure to keep it out of drafts so that it dries evenly. You may also need to cover the rim to keep it from drying faster than the bottom.

6. As soon as the rim has stiffened enough, turn the bowl over onto a soft-surfaced bat and trim the foot with your loop trimming tool. The soft rubber coating on the bat that Cynthia uses "grabs" the bowl and keeps it in place as she works (Photo 4).

4

7. To make a decorative line in the foot ring, Cynthia holds her fingernail against the ring as the wheel is turning (Photo 5).

5

8. Leaving the bowl upside down on the bat, move the bat to a comfortable location for carving. Cynthia places her bat on a banding wheel (Photo 6).

6

9. Use small wire loop trimming tools to carve the leather-hard clay as desired. The quality of the carved lines will vary according to the shape of the tool you use (Photo 7). (A variety of rounded and angled tools is available.) Leaving the bowl upside down as you carve will help you avoid pushing it out of round as you work.

7

10. When you've finished carving, turn the bowl upright and allow it to dry uncovered (Photo 8).

8

Above: **Stephen Fabrico,** ***Spiral Bowl,*** 1997
5" x 16" x 16" (12.5 x 40.5 x 40.5 cm). Porcelain; thrown in two stages, first for rough shape, then rethrown and refined after setting up overnight; carved when leather hard; sprayed glazes; reduction fired in gas kiln to cone 10; sandblasted.
Photo by Ralph Gabriner

Top right: **Jerry Conrad,** ***Garden Lantern—"Fuchsia,"*** 1997
20" x 9" x 9" (51 x 23 x 23 cm). Buff stoneware; lid and base thrown; body thrown in two pieces and joined, compressed; carved, dried for two months or more; sprayed with iron and nepheline syenite mixture and then with nepheline syenite and flint mixture; reduction fired in gas kiln to cone 9.
Photo by Doug Yaples

Right: **Rhea S. Shea,** ***Jar,*** 1996-97
16" x 10" x 10" (40.5 x 25.5 x 25.5 cm). Porcelain; thrown and carved, lid carved and pressed with added pieces of porcelain; sprayed glaze; reduction fired to cone 11. Photo by Bill Bachhuber

Top left: **Margaret Freeman Patterson, *Tripod,*** 1997
9" x 8" x 8" (23 x 20.5 x 20.5 cm). Stoneware; sides thrown without bottoms and altered, slab bottom, coiled and paddled feet, parts assembled while soft, sides incised and bellowed out; glazed; reduction fired in gas kiln to cone 10. Photo by Bart Kasten

Above: **Norm Schulman, *Teapot,*** 1980
11" x 8" x 6" (28 x 20.3 x 15 cm). Porcelain; carved, with handbuilt additions; iron saturate glaze; reduction fired in gas kiln to cone 9. Collection of Don Davis; photo by Evan Bracken

Left: **Matthew Lyon, *Deep Vessel with Crown and Handles,*** 1997
28" x 17" x 17" (71 x 43 x 43 cm). Terra-cotta earthenware; thrown in four sections, top ("crown") cut after being joined to lower three sections, extruded and rolled coils added, slab and coil handles added; incised with old comb; oxidation fired to cone 01, then smoked using torch and newspaper. Photo by Bill Bachhuber

Top right: **Sid Oakley and Brad Tucker, *Carved Bowl,*** 1997
10" x 13" x 13" (25.5 x 33 x 33 cm). Stoneware; thrown and carved; red iron oxide rubbed in and then off; reduction fired to cone 10.
Photo by Seth Tice-Lewis

Right: **Denise Woodward-Detrich, *Bowl,*** 1997
3" x 5" x 5" (7.5 x 12.5 x 12.5 cm). Porcelain; thrown, with altered lip, carved; fired in electric kiln to cone 10. Photo by artist

Bottom left: **Ronalee Herrmann and Alfred Stolken, *Untitled,*** 1997
13" x 8" x 8" (33 x 20.5 x 20.5 cm). Porcelain; thrown and shaped with a rib, carved when leather hard, sculptural additions; crystalline and non-crystalline glazes applied to bisque fired ware; fired in modified electric kiln to cone 12, light reduction with propane gas.
Photo by Alfred Stolken

Bottom right: **Peter Rose, *Carved Bottle,*** 1997
12" x 6" x 6" (30.5 x 15 x 15 cm). Porcelain; thrown; greenware carved, shino glaze on exterior; wood fired to cone 10. Photo by John Cummings

PLATE

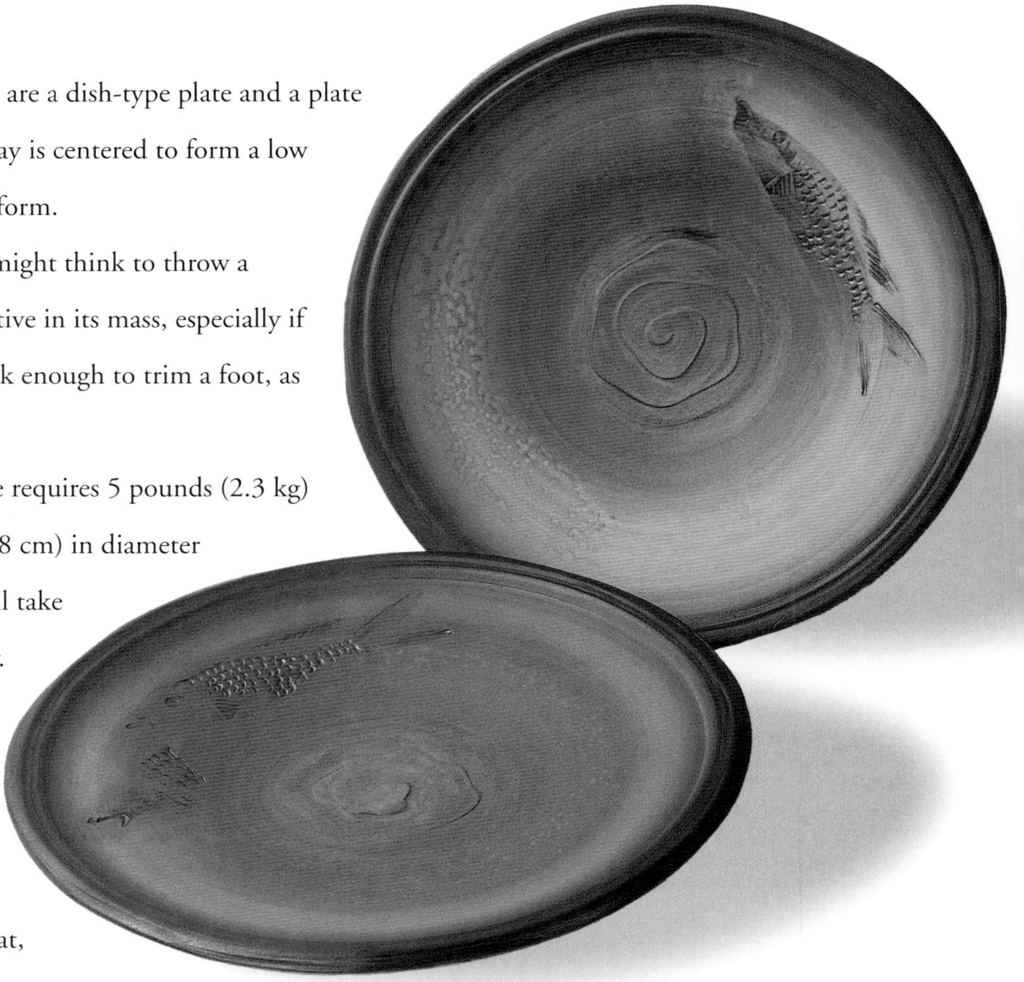

The project and variation offered here are a dish-type plate and a plate with a flared rim. In both cases, the clay is centered to form a low disk shape in order to begin the plate form.

You'll need more clay than you might think to throw a plate; its flattened shape is a bit deceptive in its mass, especially if you make the bottom of the plate thick enough to trim a foot, as will happen with this project.

Each of the plates presented here requires 5 pounds (2.3 kg) of clay, and each is about 11 inches (28 cm) in diameter after firing. A sandwich-sized plate will take 2½ to 3 pounds (1.1 to 1.4 kg) of clay. Depending on the size of the base of your plate, you may need to adjust these recommended weights. The wider the base, the more your cutoff wire will rise up as you cut it off the bat, and the more clay it will claim. If you have access to a plaster bat, it will eliminate the problem caused by cutoff wires because you won't need to cut the plate off.

Surface Treatment and Firing

Bisque fired to cone 06

Impression rubbed with iron-oxide solution, then plate dipped in copper sulfate solution. Rim sprayed with stain

Glaze fired to cone 7, light reduction in gas-fired kiln

Instructions

1. First center the clay to form a low mound shape on the wheel, positioning your hands as shown in Photo 1.
2. Now spread and lower the clay into a disk shape, using your right fist to apply pressure to the top. The heel of your left hand should prevent the clay

1

at the outer edge from folding over as it spreads and should be positioned to keep the edge sloped where the clay meets the bat (Photo 2). (Note that whenever possible, your hands should stay in contact with each other for stability.) As your fist presses down into the clay, it should establish the slight interior curve of your plate.

2

3. Using your fingers on the inside of the clay, continue opening the interior, maintaining the curve you established in step 2 as you do (Photo 3). Remember to leave the bottom thick enough to allow you to trim a foot.

3

4. When you've reached the stage at which the rim begins to extend beyond the base, begin pulling the clay out beyond the base, continuing to maintain the interior curve. The wheel should be turning quite slowly at this stage, and your right hand should be on the outside, supporting the rim as you pull (Photo 4). When the rim is as thick as desired, finalize its shape (Photo 5).

4

5

5. Refine the interior by pushing the slightly curved area of a wooden shaping rib—or any rib that suits your own style—over its surface (Photo 6). This may require several passes back and forth. As you can see in Photo 7, I use the rib to create a spiral wavy design in the clay.

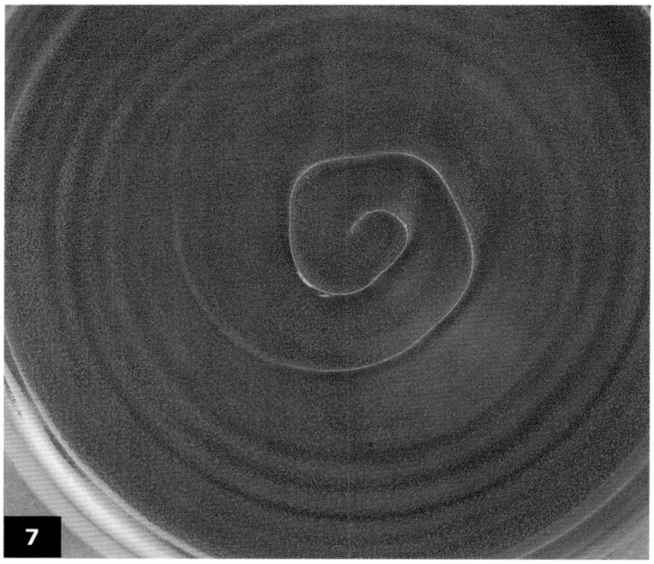

6. If you're working on a nonabsorbent bat, use your wire to separate the plate from the bat, and set the plate aside, right side up, to stiffen for trimming. (If you've thrown the plate on a plaster bat, let it stiffen without cutting it off; it will release itself.) If the rim starts to dry faster than the bottom, you may need to cover it lightly with plastic.

After this plate had stiffened a little, but was still too moist to trim, I used a clay stamp to impress it with a fish image (Photo 8). I make these stamps, with handles on their backs for ease of use, by forming the image in damp clay, then curving the clay so the image is presented on a convex surface. I bisque the stamps after they've dried.

7. This plate is trimmed in much the same way as the bowl project (see pages 60-61). First, use your trimming tool to establish the outer diameter of the foot ring. After deciding how thick the foot itself should be in order to harmonize with your plate shape, trim out the excess clay from the center bottom. Then allow the plate to dry, right side up and uncovered.

Variation

To create a plate with a flared rim, such as the one shown in the photo below, center and open the clay as before, but as you open it, make the bottom flat instead of curved. Then pull the resulting low wall outward and slightly upward, keeping it flat rather than curved and leaving a distinct definition between the flat interior and the rim (Photo 9).

Next, carefully use the straight edge of a wooden stick to flatten the rim even more. Keep the rim angled slightly upward instead of trying to make it horizontal, or it may collapse. If the clay seems soft, push the rim down almost as far as you want it to go and wait for it to stiffen a little before pushing it down farther.

As is the case with the flared bowl described on page 62, the rim will rise as it stiffens, so you'll need to push it back down before trimming. To avoid uneven drying, be sure to rotate the plate occasionally as it waits to be trimmed. If the rim is drying faster than the bottom, cover it with plastic or turn the plate upside down in order to let the bottom catch up. (Make sure the surface that the plate rests on won't mar the rim.)

When the flared plate is ready to trim, use your calipers to measure the diameter of the flat bottom (Photo 10). Then, after turning the plate upside down onto a bat, use this dimension as a gauge to determine the outer diameter of your foot ring (Photo 11).

9

10

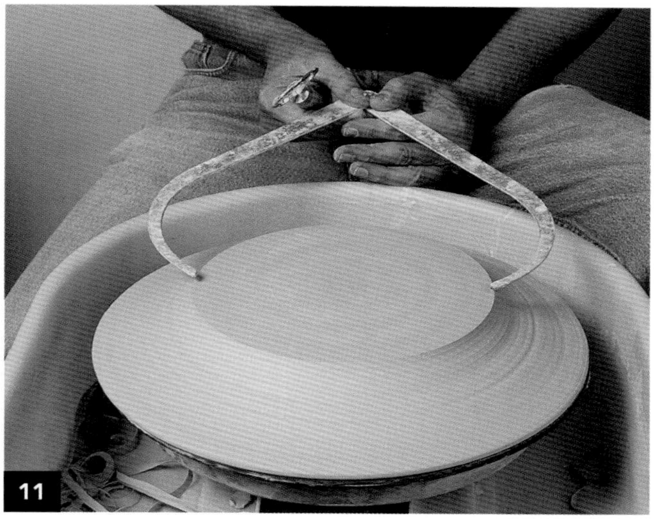
11

This will help you avoid trimming a foot that's too large and heavy, or one that's too small. (A foot that's too small can result in a rim that slumps during firing.) Now trim the foot in the same way that you trimmed the dish-type plate.

Possible Problems and Solutions

Problem: After opening, you don't have enough clay to make the flared rim as wide as you'd like.

Solution: Make a smaller rim this time. On your next plate, use more clay. Whether you're throwing a dish-type plate or one with a flared rim, the amount of clay that you have to work with after opening determines how wide the rim can be.

Problem: The interior of the foot ring (the central area at the bottom of the plate) sags down as you trim.

Solution: Turn the plate right side up and gently use the palm of your hand to press the clay back to its original shape. Then turn it upside down again and let it stiffen a bit before continuing to trim. Sagging is often caused by the clay being either too soft or too thin. In the first case, waiting longer before trimming will take care of the problem. In the second case, I recommend using more clay on your next plate.

Problem: An S-shaped crack develops in the bottom of your plate as it dries.

Solution: This cracking is fairly common in pieces with large-diameter bases because the farther the clay is opened away from the center, the weaker and less compressed the clay will be. To avoid this problem, after opening the clay, while the wheel is turning slowly, compress the clay by tamping the center area down with the side of your fist.

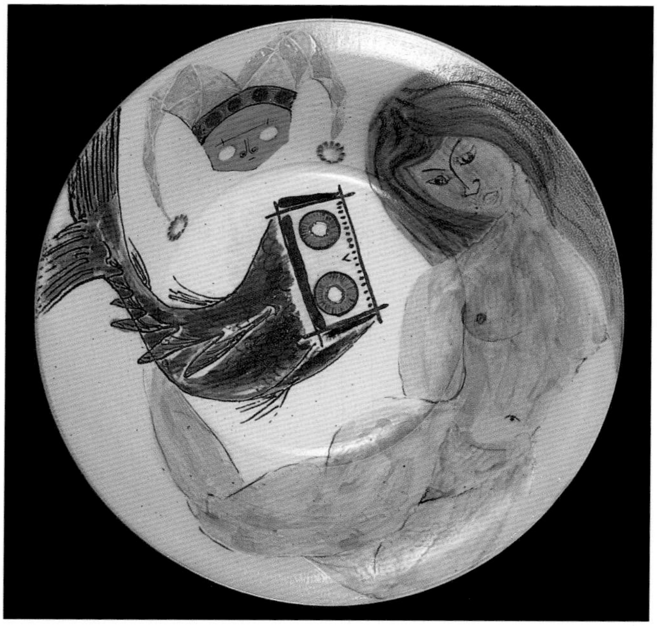

Top left: **Norm Schulman, *Charger,*** 1981
Diameter: 21" (53.5 cm). Porcelain, painted with englobes on bone-dry greenware, once fired to cone 9 in salt glaze kiln. Photo by artist

Bottom left: **Winthrop Byers, *Copper Red Platter,*** 1997
1½" x 15" x 15" (4 x 38 x 38 cm). Stoneware; thrown, rim flared with straight rib, inverted and trimmed; bisque fired in electric kiln to cone 07; sprayed glazes; fired in gas kiln to cone 11. Photo by Sandra Byers

Top right: **Steven Hill, *Platter,*** 1997
3" x 21" x 21" (7.5 x 53.5 x 53.5 cm). White stoneware; thrown, rim altered with finger, then marks accentuated with rib; trailed and brushed slips, multiple sprayed glazes; once fired, reduction, in gas kiln to cone 10. Photo by Al Surratt

Bottom right: **Anonymous, *Untitled,*** Austrian plate (circa 1850)
Diameter: 9" (23 cm). Earthenware; slip trailed, majolica-type glaze, overglaze brushwork. Photo courtesy of Glenn Rand

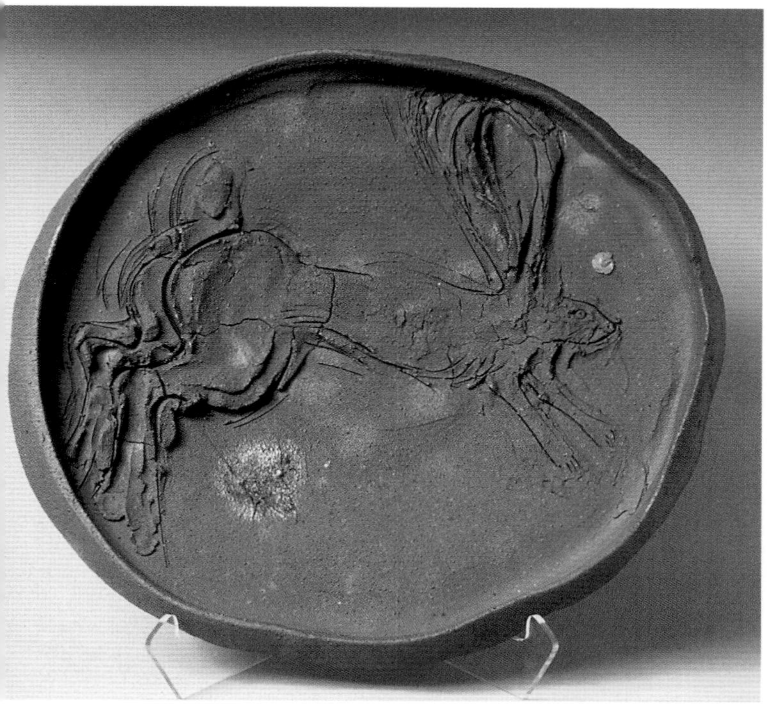

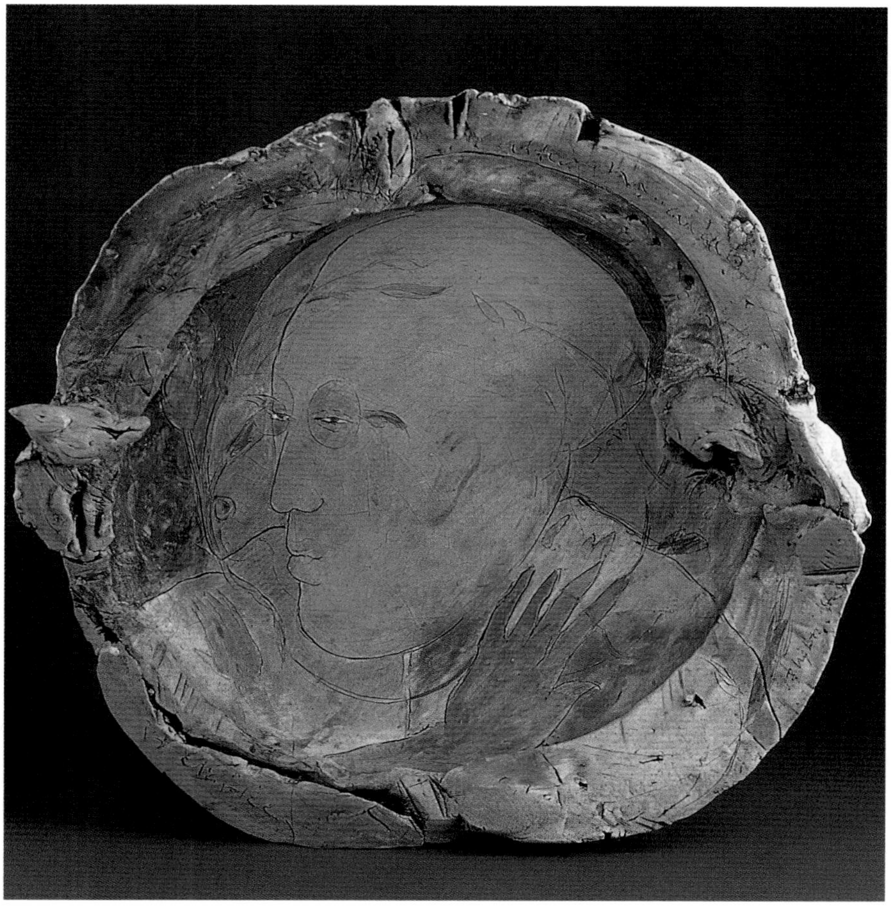

Top left: **Ken Ferguson, *Hare Platter,*** 1987
Diameter: 22" (56 cm). Black stoneware; residual salt fired; fired osage spot (hedge apple). Photo by Ken Ferguson, courtesy of Garth Clark Gallery, New York, NY

Top right: **Peter Voulkos, *Untitled,*** 1997
24" x 22½" x 5½" (61 x 57 x 14 cm). Stoneware; thrown and altered; wood-fired. Photo courtesy of Perimeter Gallery, Chicago, IL

Right: **Robert Bede Clarke, *In Return for this Jasmine Odor (after Machado),*** 1997
24" x 25" x 5" (61 x 63.5 x 12.5 cm). Earthenware; platter thrown, then moved out of round; when leather hard, slab rim and other additions attached; drawn on, carved, and trimmed; textured slip and colored engobes applied; bisque fired to cone 04; rubbed stain, light wash of frit; fired in electric kiln to cone 03

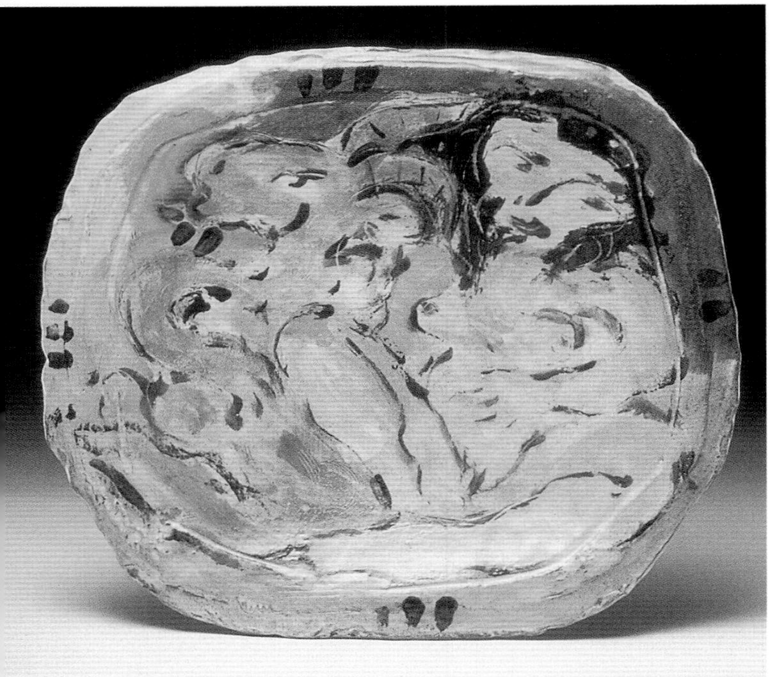

Top left: **Ron Meyers, *Platter,*** 1995
4" x 14" x 16" (10 x 35.5 x 40.5 cm). Earthenware; thrown disk, stretched while wet and draped over plaster hump mold; painted with white slip, underglazes, stains; bisque fired; transparent glaze; oxidation fired in gas kiln to cone 04. Photo by Walker Montgomery

Top right: **Don Davis, *Platter with Floating Squares,*** 1994
Diameter: 18" (45.5 cm). Porcelain; bisque fired to cone 06; underglaze oxide solutions, resist pattern, interior sprayed and painted; rim glaze trailed, sprayed with rutile solution; glaze fired to cone 9, light reduction. Photo by J. Weiland

Left: **Lucy Breslin, *Summer Song #10,*** 1996
6" x 20" x 20" (15 x 51 x 51 cm). White earthenware; platter thrown; discs and cylinders thrown, cut, folded, and assembled when leather hard; glazes brushed, resist-applied, sprayed, and rebrushed; glaze fired to cone 04. Photo by artist

Right: **Neil Patterson,** ***Oval Platter (Hale-Bopp),*** 1997
4" x 19" x 16" (10 x 48.5 x 40.5 cm). White stoneware; thrown components, textured on the wheel, flattened, and "quilted" together using a shallow slump mold; spodumene glaze with sprayed oxides; reduction fired in gas kiln to cone 10. Photo by artist

Bottom: **Mike Vatalaro,** ***Vessel/Reconstruction,*** 1997
7" x 23" x 22" (18 x 58.5 x 56 cm). White stoneware; thrown, cut when leather hard, and assembled; sprayed glaze; reduction fired in gas kiln to cone 10.
Photo by artist

▪ PITCHER

As functional pieces, pitchers provide a challenge to the potter, who must balance the dual considerations of the vessels' utility and aesthetics. Pitcher forms can vary quite a bit, but no matter what shape they take, they need to be well proportioned.

The walls must be thin enough to let you lift the pitcher easily when it's filled with liquid, yet strong enough to withstand use. The bottom mustn't be too thick or too thin. The spout should be of a size that will accommodate the volume of liquid that flows through it and must also be visually pleasing as an extension of the form. The handle should be comfortable to grip and sturdy, as well as visually suitable for your pitcher body. The negative space between the handle and body must be considered as well; it's just as important as any other aspect of the overall form.

The pitcher in this project is made with 4½ pounds (2 kg) of clay and will hold approximately 2 quarts (1.9 l) of liquid. Keep in mind that the same amount of clay in different potters' hands can yield pots of different sizes. Differences in thickness, shape, and individual style all influence the amount of clay required.

The pitcher shown here was inspired by early English shapes.

Although it's based on a simple cylindrical form, its shape, the amount of clay used to throw it, and the added handle and spout will require you to take some additional steps. As you take them, you'll learn how to "shape" the belly (or wide, rounded portion) of the pitcher, "neck in" to narrow the upper portion of the thrown form, and "pull" a spout and handle.

Pulling takes some practice, but it's a process worth learning because pulled handles provide a graceful flowing effect that is unattainable in any other way.

Before attaching additions such as the handle on this pitcher, you must let the thrown body stiffen somewhat. If the body is still too damp when you try to pick it up, it will let you know: You won't be able to hold the clay without distorting it. If you let the body dry too much before attaching the handle, the handle will crack later, so monitor the drying process closely. (Wet clay can never be successfully joined to dry clay.) When your schedule makes close monitoring impossible, cover the pitcher body with plastic until you can finish the piece.

Surface Treatment and Firing

Bisque fired to cone 06

Interior glazed; exterior sprayed with stain and oversprayed with separating glaze

Glaze fired to cone 7, light reduction in gas-fired kiln

Instructions

1. Prepare the clay by wedging it well. Pat it into a ball or cone shape and place it on the wheel. As the wheel turns very slowly, push the clay on both sides a few times to help move it into the center of the bat.
2. With the wheel turning at centering speed, cone up the clay (Photo 1).

1

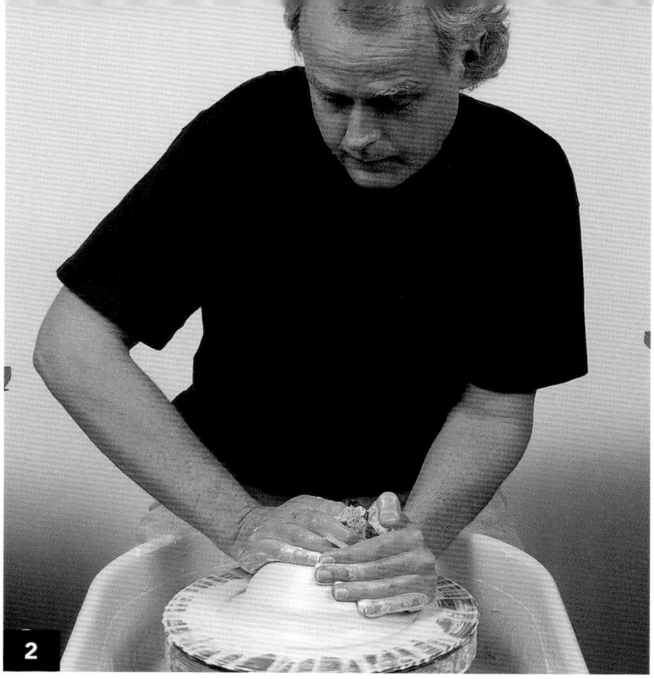
2

3. To complete the centering, push the cone down, using the hand positions shown in Photo 2. You may need to cone up and push back down a couple of times in order to center the clay.
4. Open the clay as you would for a flat-bottomed cylinder. How far you open it will roughly determine the diameter of the base of your pitcher.
5. Pull the cylinder walls, making sure to leave enough clay at the top to create a strong edge and also provide enough clay from which to pull the spout (Photos 3 and 4). If you're just beginning to throw, don't worry about shaping the belly of the pitcher yet. Experienced potters can begin to shape pieces as they're pulling, but this skill definitely requires some expertise. The more pulls it takes to raise the clay, the softer and more fatigued the clay will become, so try to bring the clay to its

3

4

final height in three or four pulls. Remember to reset the rim between pulls if necessary.

6. Before shaping the pitcher body, imagine your hands as opposing forces, one inside the cylinder and one outside. Applying more pressure to the clay with the hand that's inside the clay wall will make the wall bulge outward. Applying more pressure from the outside will push the wall inward. Whether you're pushing in or out, remember to support the clay by using your opposite hand on the other side of the clay wall.

   Shaping may be done with the tips, pads, or sides of your fingers or by pushing on the clay with a sponge or rib. (Pushing with or against a rib or sponge minimizes or eliminates finger marks in the clay.) The process of shaping usually takes several passes and requires a slow wheel speed.

   Learning the motions of shaping and how to exert the correct amount of directed force takes a good deal of practice. Focus on what it feels like to move the clay; don't be afraid of collapsing your clay form. Collapsed clay can be reused, and besides, there's always that next lump of clay waiting to be thrown!

   Start shaping the pitcher body by positioning your left hand at the interior bottom of the cylinder, just as you did when pulling. Hold a curved rib in the other hand and position it against the outer wall. Now work your way up, as if you were pulling, but instead of thinning the wall by drawing the clay upward, support the outer wall with the rib while using your inner fingers to push outward against it (Photo 5). Don't move the rib or your inner fingers all the way to the top of the form. Instead, move only high enough to shape the belly. (You may also work down in this fashion.)

5

7. The upper portion of this pitcher is necked in (or narrowed) and the pitcher top is then flared out. To create the inward curve, use the fingers and thumbs of both hands to apply pressure to the clay, moving them slowly up the cylinder as it turns on the wheel and removing them soon enough to allow the rim to remain flared (Photo 6). Make sure that your hands are wet enough to slide easily on the clay.

6

8. To finish the outer surface of the pitcher, use your rib to refine the shape of the neck and to blend this area so that its contour is a reverse of the curve of the belly (Photo 7). Blending the neck and belly is probably the most challenging part of shaping this pitcher.

7

9. Reset and smooth the rim. Using a small piece of damp chamois, as shown in Photo 8, creates a very smooth rim.

8

10. To lighten a pitcher, you may trim its lower portion while it's still on the bat. (See Photo 2 on page 93.) Now cut the pitcher off with your wire if necessary.

11. You'll shape the spout of this pitcher by pulling it, but this pulling is very different from pulling the wall of a cylinder. First, with the wheel standing still, moisten your fingers. Then position your fingers as shown in Photo 9, placing the straightened index and middle fingers of one hand inside the vessel and the thumb and finger of the other hand outside. Now move the outside fingers upward, squeezing the clay gently as you do. Repeat this motion as necessary to shape the spout.

Pulling a spout in this manner is usually done immediately after throwing, but if your clay is too soft and floppy to allow you to shape it as you like, let the body dry for about 30 minutes before continuing. (You'll need to monitor the piece closely as it dries. As you know, temperature and humidity influence drying times a great deal.)

12. Finish the pulled portion of the spout by rounding off its lip with one finger (Photo 10). The edge of the spout should be fairly sharp. If it's too round, when you tilt the pitcher back up after pouring, it won't cut off the flow of liquid quickly enough to prevent dripping. When the pitcher is upright, the spout should also tilt slightly upward, or you'll encounter the same problem with dripping.

13. Allow the pitcher to stiffen somewhat. Cover the top once it reaches leather hard so it won't dry out before the lower portion. This will take several hours—possibly even overnight. When the clay is stiff enough to handle, finish its bottom by rolling the bottom edge on a clean work surface and smoothing the beveled edge with one finger.

9

10

14. To make the pulled handle, start by thoroughly wedging a piece of clay. (Clay that will be pulled must be even in consistency and free of lumps.)

15. Pat the wedged clay into a cone shape. Then hold the clay up so that you can see what you're doing (Photo 11), dip your free hand in water, and wet the clay with your hand.

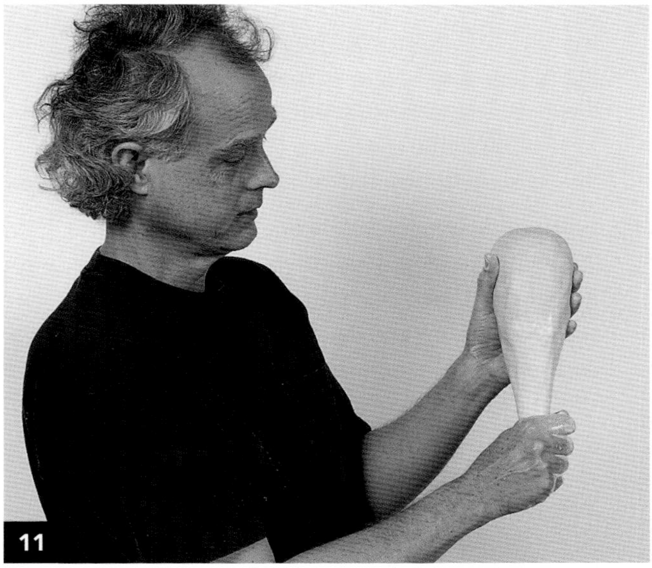

11

16. To pull the clay (a gradual process), cup your wetted hand around the upper portion of the clay and slip your hand downward, right past the clay's tapered end. Your goal here is to taper the clay by gradually closing your fingers as they slip downward. As you do this, don't squeeze the clay hard; exert just enough pressure to shape the clay slightly in the hollow between your thumb and index finger. Keep the taper even by switching from one side of the clay to the other with each pull. This will help prevent you from shaping a handle that's thicker on one side than on the other.

17. Take a look at Photo 12. When you've pulled a nub about the size of the one shown, set the clay on the edge of your work surface and cut the nub off. Making this nub will only take a few pulls—perhaps six or seven.

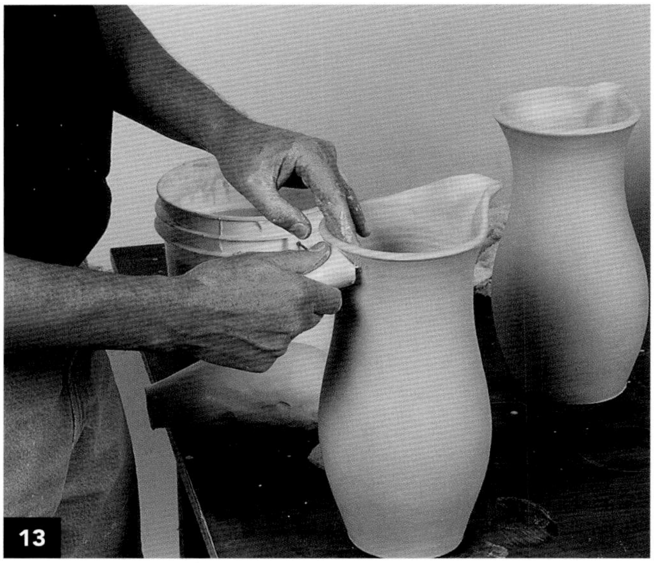

13

12

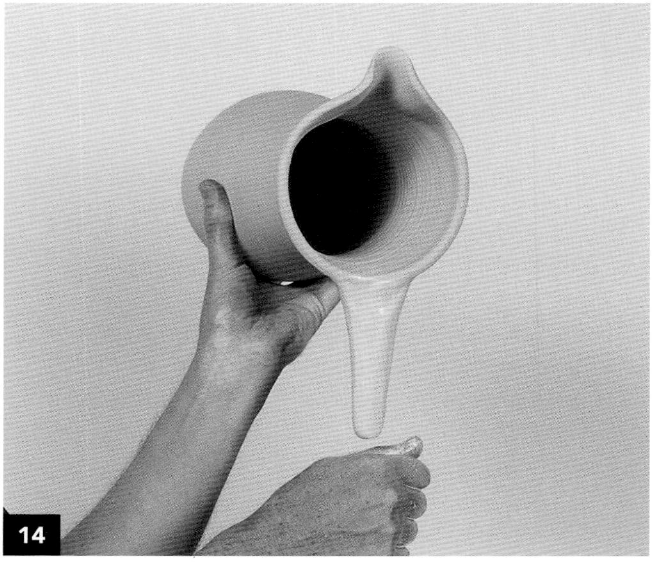

14

18. Score the fat end of the nub and the portion of the pitcher where you intend to attach it. Apply slurry or water to the scored portion of the nub. Then, holding the nub with your thumb and index finger, press the nub onto the pitcher (Photo 13). Smooth the moist clay to secure the nub in place.

19. Holding the pitcher as shown in Photos 14 and 15, continue to pull the handle so that it flows pleasingly from the form. Don't forget to alternate your pulling, working on one side of the handle and then on the other. Also remember to continue each stroke slightly past the end of the clay. This will help prevent an unwanted bulb from forming at the end of the clay and will result in a handle that tapers both in thickness and in width.

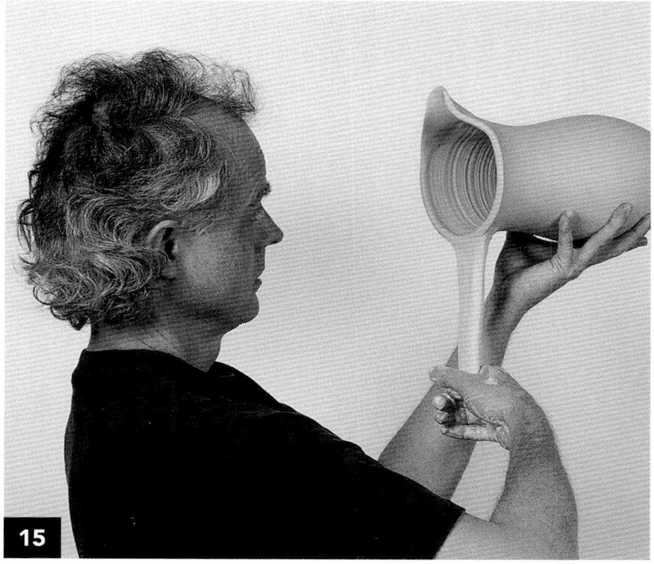

15

20. When you've formed a handle that's a little longer than necessary and that complements the shape of your pitcher, lower the pitcher carefully onto your work surface (Photo 16).

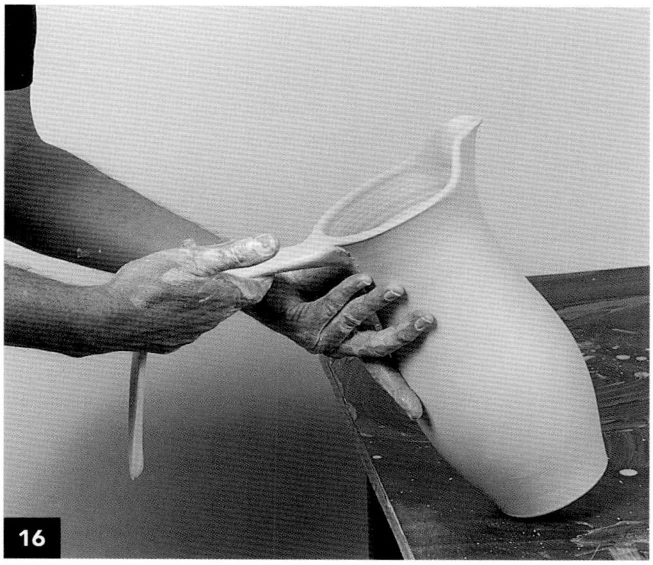

16

21. Gently supporting the handle with one hand, loop it downward, check the shape that you've formed with it, and pinch off any excess clay to correct the length. Now score and apply slurry or water to the area on the pitcher where the end of the handle will be placed and use one finger to press the handle in place (Photo 17). This will leave a single, fresh finger dent. You may want to smooth the bottom end of the handle into the pitcher for a different effect.

17

22. Unless you've overworked and softened the handle during pulling, it will hold its shape fairly well as it stiffens. To adjust its position, first let it stiffen a bit. Then make any final adjustments and smooth away any rough spots with a damp sponge.

23. Cover the pitcher with a thin sheet of plastic for a day or two to prevent it from drying too quickly. When pieces of clay are joined, they need this time alone to get acquainted and also to let moisture differences between them equalize, or the clay may crack.

Variations

You can pull a handle separately and let it stiffen to shape by draping it over a 5-gallon (1.9 l) bucket covered with newsprint. (The newsprint will prevent the clay from sticking.) When the handle has stiffened, score and attach it to your leather-hard vessel.

You may also make a coiled handle by simply rolling out a tapered coil on a table surface and adding it to the vessel. Extruded handles work well, too. Some potters use extruders to make the basic handle forms and then pull them to finalize and taper the shape.

Making a more pronounced spout requires adding more clay—and waiting time. Throw your pitcher first and allow the rim to stiffen a bit. Then shape a small crescent of moist clay. Score the edge of the crescent that you'll attach to the pitcher's rim (Photo 18). Also score the rim. Apply some slurry or water to the scored area of the clay crescent. Then, gingerly but thoroughly press the crescent onto the rim and blend

18

it in well (Photo 19). Next, using one hand, pull a spout where you've added the clay, using your thumb on the inside to pull against your curved index finger on the outside (Photo 20). Smooth the rim and make final adjustments as desired (Photo 21).

Possible Problems and Solutions

Problem: After shaping the body of the pitcher, the form is no longer centered on the wheel.

Solution: At this stage, none! Next time you try shaping, spin your wheel more slowly, keep the clay and your hands moist, apply less pressure, and try to apply the pressure evenly. Using slightly stiffer clay may also help.

Problem: The rib bounces or chatters on the clay as you try to shape the cylinder.

Solution: Adjust the angle at which you're holding the rib.

Problem: During shaping, you have difficulty aligning the fingers of one hand with the fingers of the other hand or with the rib.

Solution: Push very gently from the inside of the piece and watch for the slight bulge on the outside. Then place your fingers or rib at that location.

Problem: The area you're necking in wrinkles as it narrows.

Solution: The clay wall in that area may be too thin or too wet and soft. Slow down the wheel and apply the pressure more gently. If you catch this problem early enough, you may be able to even the clay by starting below the wrinkle and working up into it. If this doesn't work, it may be easier to try again on your next pitcher rather than struggle with this one. Next time, try using stiffer clay.

Problem: After necking in, the rim is uneven.

Solution: Use a needle tool to cut off the uneven portion (see page 40).

Problem: Your added handle droops so much that it won't hold a shape.

Solution: Holding the handle in the desired position, drape a wet strip of newsprint or paper towel from the inner rim of the pitcher, down the length of the handle. This will help hold the handle in place until it stiffens enough to stay put. If the pitcher has a very sturdy rim and spout, setting it upside down for a while is another alternative that may help.

19

20

21

Top left: **Will Ruggles and Douglass Rankin,** ***Pitcher,*** 1995
11½" x 6½" x 6" (29 x 16.5 x 15 cm). White stoneware; thrown, with added handle; slip dipped and finger-wiped, glaze dots, iron stripes; wood fired in three-chambered noborigama-style kiln until cone 9 had bent halfway down, light salt and soda additions.
Photo by Will Ruggles

Top right: **Robert Bede Clarke,** ***Minoan,*** 1996
20" x 15" x 15" (51 x 38 x 38 cm). Earthenware; body thrown right-side-up and shoulder torch-dried; body then inverted in chuck and thrown in reverse direction to allow for narrow base; slab base added; neck and handle added when piece stiff; line drawing and colored engobes; bisque fired to cone 05; rubbed stain; saggar fired to cone 08

Right: **Ellen Shankin,** ***Pitcher,*** 1997
11" x 6" (28 x 15 cm). Stoneware; thrown and faceted with Surform; fake ash glaze; reduction fired in gas kiln to cone 9

Top left: **Don Davis,** ***Tripod Pitcher,*** 1997
Height: 12" (30.5 cm). Porcelain; bisque fired to 06; thrown body and thrown, added feet; sprayed engobe with tape-resist pattern; glaze fired to cone 7, light reduction. Photo by Tim Barnwell

Top right: **Brad Tucker,** ***Pitcher,*** 1996
12½" x 7" x 7" (32 x 18 x 18 cm). Stoneware; thrown, with pulled spout; oxide, slip trailed, ash glazed; reduction fired to cone 10

Left: **Vernon Owens,** Jugtown Pottery, 1997
7" x 4½" x 4½" (18 x 11.5 x 11.5 cm). Stoneware; pulled strap handle; bisque fired; liner glaze applied to interior; salt glazed to cone 10 in wood-fired groundhog kiln. Collection of Don Davis; photo by Evan Bracken

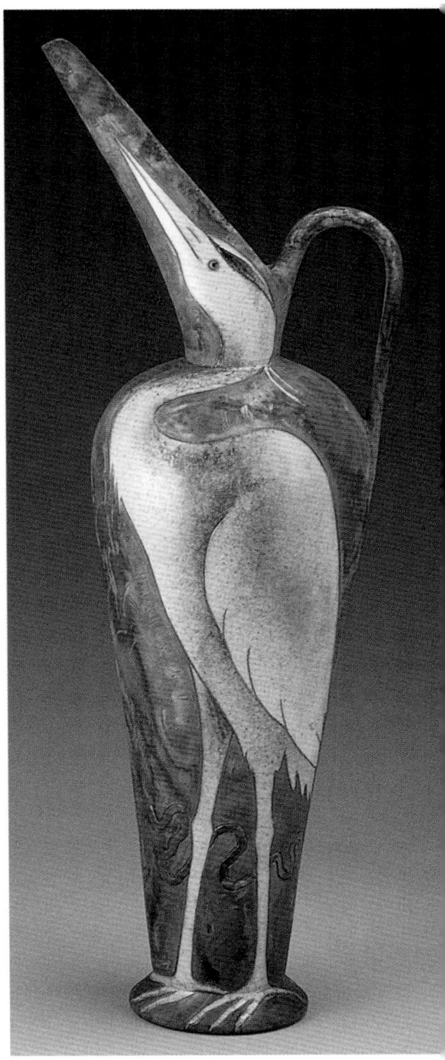

Top left: **Beth Thomas,** ***Seven Sisters Ewer,*** 1996
22" x 9" x 9" (56 x 23 x 23 cm). Earthenware; parts thrown, cut, and assembled (stacked at leather-hard stage); terra sigillata slip, hand burnished; wrapped in salt-water-soaked grasses, saggar fired in gas kiln to cone 010. Photo by Tracy Hicks

Top center: **Shane M. Keena,** ***Meristematic Ewer,*** 1997
15" x 9¼" x 10" (38 x 23.5 x 25.5 cm). Earthenware (mixed dark and white); thrown and altered by squeezing and twisting, scraped, hand-built and slip-cast additions, sanded; bisque fired in electric kiln to cone 04; glazes, Barnard clay applied as a stain; glaze fired to cone 06; commercial wood stain and paint brush hair. Photo by Kevin Koppers

Top right: **Dave and Boni Deal,** ***Egret Ewer,*** 1997
24" x 12" x 8" (61 x 30.5 x 20.5 cm). Raku; body thrown; neck thrown, cut, and smoothed; handle pulled; clay etched with pencil, background brush-textured with dry matt stain; glazed, masked, shaded with oxides; raku fired to cone 06. Photo by Bill Bachhuber

Right: **Laura Saville,** ***Oval Pitcher,*** 1997
9" x 11" x 5" (23 x 28 x 12.5 cm). Earthenware; body thrown, inverted, and oval section removed from base; hole squeezed closed to form oval, bottom ribbed smooth, spout cut from separate thrown pot; underglazes; clear glaze; rapidly fired to cone 06. Photo by Azad

Wavy Oval Vase

In this project, I'll introduce some altering methods for the rim and body of a piece. Although this vase begins as a simple cylindrical shape, there are endless possibilities for subtle variarions in its simple form.

After potters master basic throwing techniques, they can begin to let go of some control and let the clay speak through. Each potter's personality will guide him or her to seek a comfortable level of "give and take" with the clay. I'm not what's considered to be a "loose" thrower. The vase treatment I present here is particularly well suited to my own sensibilities, as it sets up a situation in which the clay grows in its own loose manner on a portion of the piece, leaving the rest in my hands. I developed this technique to allow myself to give up some control to the clay. I use about 5 to 7 pounds (2.3 to 3.2 kg) of clay to throw one of these vases and, as I do with all my forms, I throw several in one day.

Surface Treatment and Firing

Exterior: see steps 10-12

Bisque fired to cone 06

Interior glazed; exterior sprayed with oxide solutions

Glaze fired (oxidation) to cone 6

Instructions

1. Center and open the clay for a flat-bottomed cylinder. When you're making vertically oriented forms, leaving a little extra thickness at the bottom of the cylinder wall will give the pot the strength to stand up as you pull the walls. (The larger the piece, the more this will help). After the final shaping, you'll trim the extra clay to the desired dimension in order to avoid ending up with a bottom-heavy piece. Using fairly stiff clay will also help you achieve a lightweight, tall form.

2. Make the first pull. Then use a pear-shaped trimming tool to remove small scoops of clay from the rim (Photo 1). For subtle variations in the final

1

effects, you may also cut the scoops with a knife, cut them at different angles, or cut them earlier or later in the pulling process.

3. Pull up and shape the walls, leaving the rim as undisturbed as possible and allowing it to undulate as it will to create a soft, wavy rim. Throwing this way—letting the clay take part of the control—is an exhilarating challenge.

4. Take the flexible steel rib all the way up the outside of the piece during the final shaping, in order to help create a fairly thin rim.

5. You may trim this pot, if necessary, right after throwing, while it's still moist and upright on the wheel (Photo 2).

2

6. Rib the piece smooth again. Then separate it from the bat, if necessary, and either leave it on the bat to stiffen for a bit, or remove it and set it on a ware board, banding wheel, or table top.

7. After the form has stiffened a little but is still flexible, start altering it by pressing it between your hands to create an oval shape (Photo 3). Then work on it more by pushing in its walls every hour or so throughout the day to achieve the final shape as the clay continues to stiffen. The clay will only accept a certain amount of altering at a time because it tends to spring back toward its original round shape after you push on it. (The wetter the clay, the more it will spring back.) As it stiffens, it will cooperate with you more each time you push it.

8. I also make a vertical dent in this vase, using the heels of my hands. Make sure your hands are clean and dry when you press the clay in this manner. If the clay is sticky to the touch, it needs to stiffen a bit more. Watch it carefully, however; if it dries too much, it will crack when you reshape it, especially at the rim. If you have to leave the pot for any length of time, cover it with thin plastic to slow down the drying process.

3

9. After the piece has stiffened to leather hard and will hold its new shape, run a small sponge around the wavy rim to eliminate any sharp edges.

10. The paper-resist technique that I used on this piece is relatively easy. Right after altering, start by tearing sheets of newsprint, dipping them in water, and sticking them onto the leather-hard clay (Photo 4). The way in which you arrange the strips offers great design possibilities. I aim for a

4

balance of tension and harmony between the design and the form. I tear the newsprint because the torn, uneven edges relate to the uneven rim and overall feeling of the piece. Many variations on this technique are possible, including cutting the paper into intricate shapes with a pair of scissors or the blade of a craft knife. Try the variations that seem most appropriate for your own pieces.

11. Brush the entire vase with an engobe the color of which will contrast with the fired color of your clay.

12. Wait for the engobe to dry from shiny to matt. Then peel the paper off by lifting the edges with the pointed end of a needle tool and pulling the paper strips away with your fingers (Photo 5). If you have trouble seeing the paper strips under the engobe, shine a light directly onto the pot to help you locate them. I leave the outer surfaces of these pieces unglazed and spray metallic colorant solutions into the resist areas left by the paper. For some potentially rich effects, you may also apply any transparent glaze over the exterior after bisque firing.

5

Variations

The vases shown in the photo above were shaped with a Surform rasp. These tools come in a variety of shapes and sizes and are great for shaping leather-hard clay. Start by throwing the basic form, leaving the clay a little thicker than usual. Push the form into an oval shape and allow it to stiffen somewhat. Then use the rasp in much the same way as you'd use a cheese grater on a chunk of cheddar (Photo 6). The tool leaves a texture that can provide a pleasing

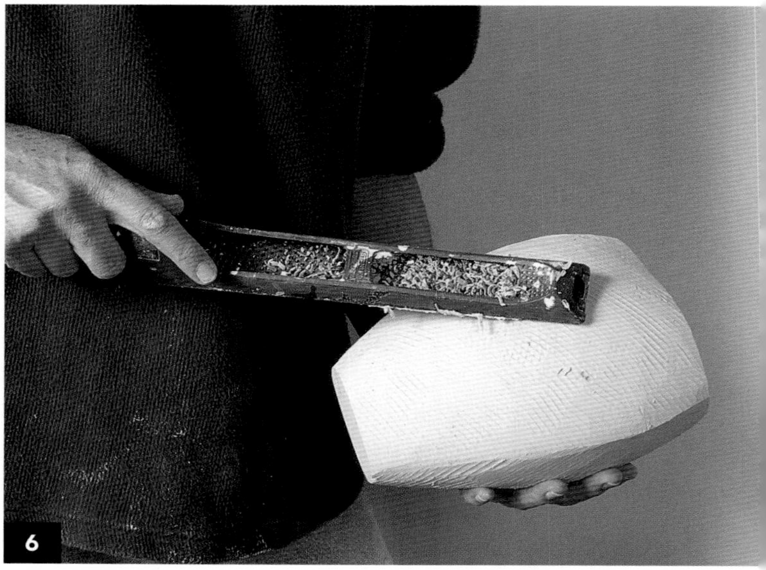

6

design feature. If the texture is a distraction to you, scrape it off with a metal rib.

I use this rasp during two phases of shaping. When the clay is at the soft stage of leather hard, I use it to rough in the desired form and edges. After the clay has stiffened a bit more, I use the tool again to finalize the shape and to give the edges their final crispness. You'll be able to tell when the clay is at the right stage for Surform work when the tool shaves the clay off easily without sticking.

Complete the rim treatment on this piece after shaping the form to your satisfaction. Use a fettling knife to cut it freely into a wavy shape (Photo 7). Then wipe the rim with a small elephant ear sponge to eliminate any sharp edges.

7

Possible Problems and Solutions

Problem: The pot cracks when you try to push it into an oval shape.

Solution: None. Your clay probably wasn't flexible enough or wedged well enough, or the form dried too long. If the problem persists even when you use well-wedged clay, try a more plastic clay body. Also monitor the drying process carefully.

Problem: When you try to use the Surform, clay gums up in it.

Solution: Let the clay stiffen a bit longer before trying again.

Problem: The Surform just scrapes the surface of the pot and doesn't remove much clay.

Solution: Replace the blade (it can't be resharpened). If the pot has stiffened too much to shave successfully, making a new pot may be easier and more productive than struggling with one that's too dry.

Problem: Engobe seeps under the paper resist and mars your design.

Solution: Wait until the piece dries. Then carefully scrape the unwanted engobe away with a blade. Next time you use this paper-resist technique, make sure to wet the paper completely and stick it securely onto the pot before applying the engobe.

Top: **Ruri,** ***Play of Winds,*** 1988
9½" x 5" x 24" (24 x 12.5 x 61 cm). Porcelain; thrown, squeezed when soft leather hard, sides cut; slip-soaked rice paper applied when stiff leather hard; bisque fired; sprayed with matt glaze; reduction fired in gas kiln to cone 11

Left: **Chris Hill,** ***Swirl Bottle,*** 1996
22" x 10" x 10" (56 x 25.5 x 25.5 cm). Stoneware; thrown in sections, segmented, assembled; hand-rolled horns; lines impressed when leather hard; sprayed ash glaze on body, iron saturate glaze on neck; reduction fired in gas kiln to cone 9-10. Photo by Tim Barnwell

Center: **Maggie Creshkoff,** ***White Vessel,*** 1996
7" x 6" x 6" (18 x 15 x 15 cm). Red stoneware; thrown on kick wheel, stamped with carved wooden stamp; cut, stretched, and paddled to make feet; white slip applied; fired in oil-burning kiln to cone 6. Photo by Bobby Hansson

Top left: **Sandra Byers, *Cincinnus,*** 1997
3½" x 2⅜" x 2¼" (9 x 6 x 5.5 cm). Porcelain; thrown, foot trimmed, dampened, triangular extrusions added; cut, pinched, carved, and incised in repeated steps; bisque fired in electric kiln to cone 04; microcrystalline matt glaze with manganese carbonate; oxidation glaze fired to cone 9½. Photo by artist

Bottom left: **Ian Stainton, *Altered Vase #1,*** 1997
15" x 8" x 8" (38 x 20.5 x 20.5 cm). Porcelain; thrown, altered by pushing from inside; carved exterior, reduction fired to cone 10. Photo by Bruce Cramer

Top right: **Ginny Conrow, *Yawning Vase,*** 1997
6½" x 3½" x 3½" (16.5 x 9 x 9 cm). Porcelain; thrown, cut, and altered; sprayed crystalline glazes; fired in electric kiln to cone 10. Photo by Roger Schreiber

Bottom right: **Shiho Kanzaki, *Iga Vase,*** 1996
10" x 5" x 5" (25.5 x 12.5 x 12.5 cm). "Gairome" clay (primary ingredients kaolin and quartz granules) dug from a mountainside by the potter; coiled, then thrown just once; fired for ten days in anagama kiln. Photo courtesy of Dick Lehman

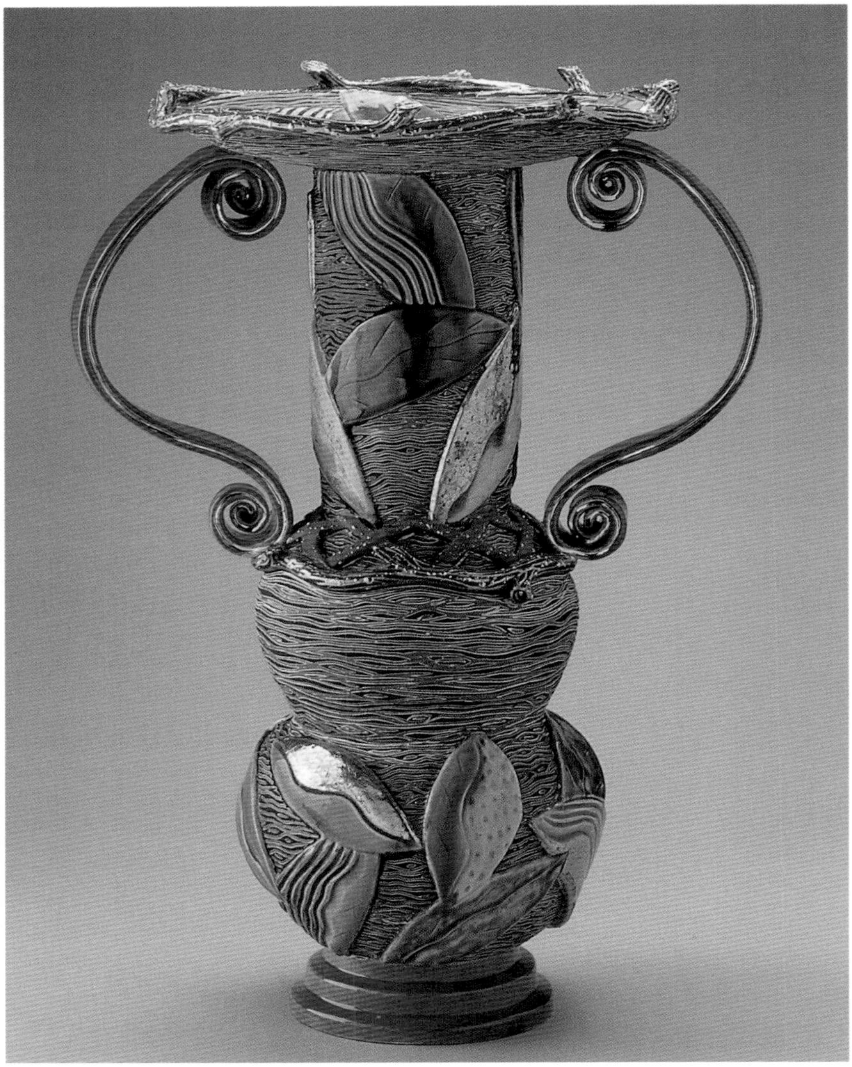

Top left: **Annette Siffin,** ***Vase,*** 1996
9½" x 11" x 5½" (24 x 28 x 14 cm). Lower body thrown and altered, upper body thrown and hump molded, body assembled, three necks added; fake ash glaze; reduction fired in gas kiln to cone 10. Photo by Christopher Campbell

Top right: **Geert Lap,** ***Blue Vase,*** 1991
8" x 11½" x 11½" (20.5 x 29 x 29 cm). Stoneware; burnished terra sigillata.
Photo courtesy of Garth Clark Gallery, New York, NY

Left: **Carol Gouthro,** ***Vase #3,*** 1997
24" x 17" x 13" (61 x 43 x 33 cm). Terra-cotta; thrown in four sections, top as bowl shape, middle as cylinder, and bottom two as spheres; carved and attached when leather hard, base slip-cast and attached, coiled and slab-built additions; slips, underglazes (sgraffito), layered glazes, and lusters; bisque fired in electric kiln to cone 04; glaze fired to cone 05; luster fired to cone 018. Photo by Roger Schreiber

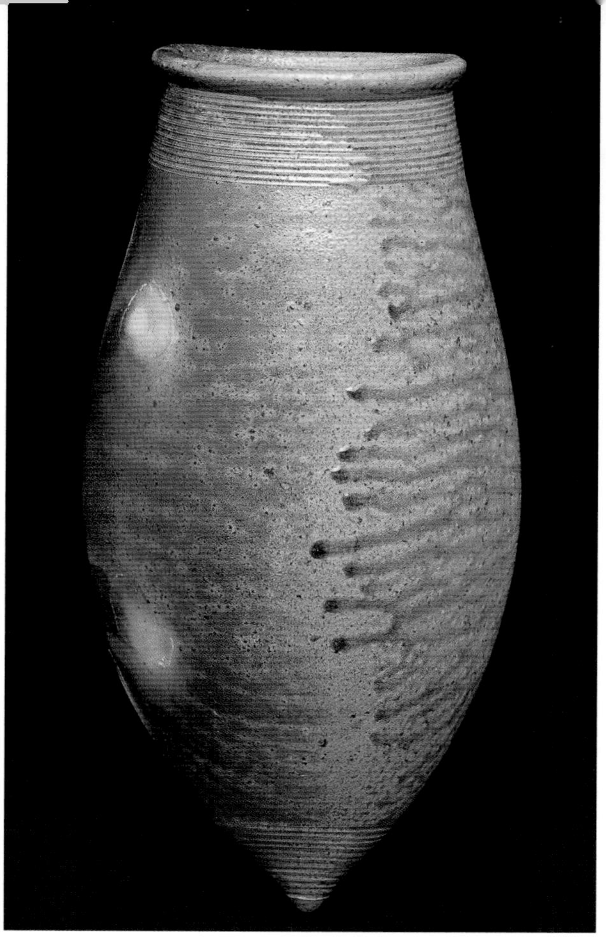

Top left: **Mark Hewitt, *Wall Vase,*** 1996
Height: 14" (35.5 cm). Stoneware; thrown upside down without a base, then laid flat on its back; wood-fired on its side, salt glazed

Top right: **Charles Fergus Binns (1857-1934), *Bronze-Form Vase,*** 1931
Height: 7⅝" (19.6 cm). Stoneware; glazed. Charles Binns is considered to be the "father" of American studio ceramics. Courtesy of the International Museum of Ceramic Art, New York State College of Ceramics at Alfred University, Alfred, NY

Right: **Val Cushing, *Floor Vase***
Height: 28" (71 cm). Stoneware; thrown in two sections; chrome slip: fired to cone 9 in gas kiln

■ TEAPOT

Making teapots is certainly one of the greatest challenges a potter can take on. Although combining their different elements—the body, spout, lid, and handle—offers many wonderful design possibilities, it also presents the opportunity to create visual incongruity. While a certain amount of visual tension can be exciting, the various elements of a teapot do need to work together as a whole.

Before you begin, study some teapots that you admire, paying particular attention to the proportional relationship between the body and the parts added to it. Also try using a few teapots to see how well they function. Nonfunctional teapots are quite a trend, but this project deals with the elements of making one that will work when it's used. The dual challenges of providing both utility and visual excitement in a piece has held my interest for many years.

Several techniques are demonstrated in the following instructions: throwing a round form, throwing "off the hump" (throwing several pieces from one large piece of clay), measuring for and fitting a lid, necking in to form the spout, trimming the lid in place on the pot, trimming the bottom by placing the piece in a chuck, adding hand-built feet, and assembling the pieces.

The teapot presented here is not directly inspired by any particular precedent. The body is a round melon shape and is given "lift" by the tripod feet. (Tripod feet were often used in Native American and prehistoric European vessels.) The handle loops extravagantly over the top, framing the lid and mirroring the roundness of the body. The knob on the lid reflects the form of the feet. The bulb at the base of the spout serves as a transition from the body to the narrowed tip of the spout.

This teapot is made with 2½ pounds (1.1 kg) of clay and holds about 1 quart (.9 l) of liquid after firing.

Surface Treatment and Firing

Bisque fired to cone 06

Interior glazed

Exterior sprayed with engobe; trailed over with a separating glaze

Glaze fired to cone 7, gas-fired kiln

Instructions

1. After centering the clay on the wheel, open it so that its interior is bowl shaped.

2. Next, start pulling up the wall, beginning to shape it into a rounded form as you pull. As you work, leave as small an opening at the top as possible. Once a pot is widened at the top, it's difficult to narrow it again. To help the clay bulge out in the middle, angle both hands out as you pull the lower portion and then back in as you pull the upper portion. This won't be as easy as it sounds, but once you get the hang of it, pulling in this fashion is a more direct way to produce a round form than starting with a cylinder.

3. When the clay is almost as thin as desired and the opening is barely large enough to allow your hand to enter the pot, finish shaping the bottom half while you can still reach it by pushing out against a curved rib. (After this stage, the opening in the form will become too narrow for you to fit your entire hand inside.)

4. Finish shaping the top portion of the pot by inserting only your fingers into the opening (Photo 1). Push inward with the rib, with the pressure just above the inside finger as that finger moves up. Ribbing will thin the clay a little more, and the upper portion of the pot and the opening in it will become narrower as you do this. As you complete the final shaping, only two or three of your fingers will fit inside the form.

5. Smooth the rim with a chamois or a small, smooth sponge. Cut the form off with a wire if necessary and leave it in place on the bat. I throw several teapot bodies at one time, before I make the lids and spouts.

6. To make a lid that will fit correctly, you must measure the opening in the body with calipers (Photo 2). Then refer to Photo 3. At the top of the large piece of clay shown, I've centered a small doorknob-shaped piece in preparation for throwing off the hump. This is the process of throwing several small forms, one at a time, from a large piece of clay.

1

2

3

The beauty of this technique is that the large lump of clay doesn't have to be perfectly centered. Instead, you center a small portion at its top, throw that portion, cut it off, and squeeze up the next small portion, centering it as you do.

Throwing off the hump is an ideal way to make small cups and bowls, as well as parts for teapots, as long as the bottom diameter of each one isn't much greater than 2 inches (5 cm). A precautionary note: When you're throwing cups or bowls off the hump, after opening, tamp the inside bottom with the butt of a knife handle or trimming tool in order to compress the clay. This will help prevent S-shaped cracks from developing as the forms dry.

7. After centering a small portion of the clay, use Photo 4 as a guide to begin forming the knob for the teapot lid by using your fingers and thumbs to push the clay down. Leave some clay in the center to form the knob.

4

8. With the wheel turning slowly, finish shaping the knob as desired. I use my little finger to form a spiral groove in the knob as well, supporting the clay underneath the knob with my fingers (Photo 5).

9. Before you pull the rim out, form the part of the lid that will fit down into the teapot by using your middle finger to push up on the clay from underneath. To make sure this lower portion isn't too small for the teapot opening, check its diameter with calipers.

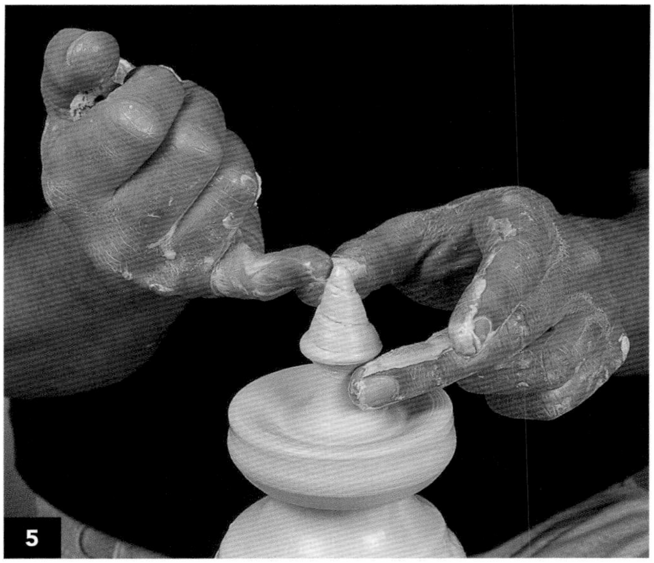

5

10. To form the flared rim of the lid, pull the clay out and slightly upward, flattening it with your fingers as you do (Photo 6).

6

11. Using calipers, measure the bottom portion of the lid again (Photo 7). It must fit into the teapot opening, but its diameter should be a bit larger than necessary at this stage so that you can trim it for a perfect fit later.

12. To separate the lid from the hump, first use a wooden stick to make a groove at its base (Photo 8). Then, using the groove as a guide for your cutoff wire, slice the lid off the hump (Photo 9). Carefully lift the lid up, touching its bottom portion only, and place it on a ware board next to the wheel. If it begins to dry faster than the teapot body, cover it with plastic.

7

8

9

I strongly recommend making a few extra lids, varying the knob sizes so that you'll be able to choose the lid that makes the most visual sense with the pot you've thrown.

13. Now for the spout. First, center the clay at the top of the hump that remains on the bat, forming it into a cone shape. Hollow out this cone by pushing a finger down into the centered top of the clay (Photo 10). Then pull the spout up once,

10

with one finger of the left hand on the inside and one right-hand finger on the outside. (Use the fingers most comfortable for you. I prefer to use my index finger inside and my middle finger outside.)

14. Now neck in (or narrow) the cylinder you're pulling by gradually squeezing the clay between the middle fingers and thumbs of both hands as they move upward together (Photo 11).

11

15. Continue to alternate pulling and necking in. When the opening in the spout becomes too small to insert a finger for pulling, insert the handle of a needle tool into the opening and use it as a substitute for a finger (Photo 12). Experienced potters can neck in as they pull up by exerting more pressure on the outside than on the inside.

12

16. Finalize the shape of the spout, using your fingers on the upper portion and a rib on the lower portion. Then cut the spout off the hump, just as you cut off the lid, and set it aside to dry. Watch spouts carefully during drying and cover them as soon as they're no longer sticky to the touch. A spout will dry faster than any other part you've thrown for this teapot.

Subtle differences in spout shapes can make a big difference in the look of the pot once the selected spout is attached. Because it's a common tendency to make spouts too large, I recommend making several, varying their lengths and diameters a bit, and then choosing the one that best suits your teapot body.

17. After the lid and body have stiffened enough to trim, place the lid on the body, upside down. With the wheel turning slowly, tap the lid to center it. Then trim its flat base. The leather-hard lid should stick to the body just enough to stay in place as you work (Photo 13), and even if you've cut the body from the bat, the body should stick to the moist clay underneath it. To make sure the lid doesn't pop off, use the fingers of your left hand to press down on it lightly as you trim.

13

18. Also trim the portion of the lid that will fit into the teapot opening, decreasing its diameter enough to ensure a good fit. Remember that the lid must have a slight amount of play; it shouldn't fit tightly. To check the lid, turn it over and place it into the opening in the body (Photo 14). If necessary, turn the lid upside down again, recenter it on the body, and trim away more clay.

14

19. To smooth and compress the clay on the lid's base, pass the rounded end of a wooden stick over it (Photo 15). Also use a hollow tube hole punch or a fettling knife to make a small hole in the lid; if air can't displace liquid from the pot during pouring, the teapot won't pour well. (To use the knife, just twist its tip as you push it through the clay.)

15

20. Center a greenware chuck on the wheel head or bat, place the teapot body in the chuck, upside down, and adjust the body to center it. Then round the base by trimming away the excess clay in that area (Photo 16). The body walls should be consistent in thickness when you're finished. Rib the trimmed area to smooth and compress the clay (Photo 17).

21. To begin making the teapot's three feet, hand-form three balls of clay, all the same size, and shape them into cones. (I sometimes throw these cones off the hump, as closed forms.) Twist each cone with your fingers to achieve the spiral effect shown in Photo 18. When the base of the pot has stiffened somewhat, mark a spot for each foot on its base. Then score and apply a little slurry to the flat base of each leg and to the spots marked on the pot. Position the legs, spacing them evenly, on the base of the pot and press them in place (Photo 19). Be careful: If the bottom isn't stiff enough, you may dent it when you press down the legs.

22. When the legs have stiffened enough to support the body, remove the body from the chuck and place it upright on your work surface. If the teapot isn't level, simply push down gently on its top to adjust it. The legs should still be soft enough to compress a little as you do this.

23. One at a time, hold up the spouts, positioning them on the teapot body, and choose the best one. Hold this spout in place on the body, making sure that its tip will be above the surface of

16

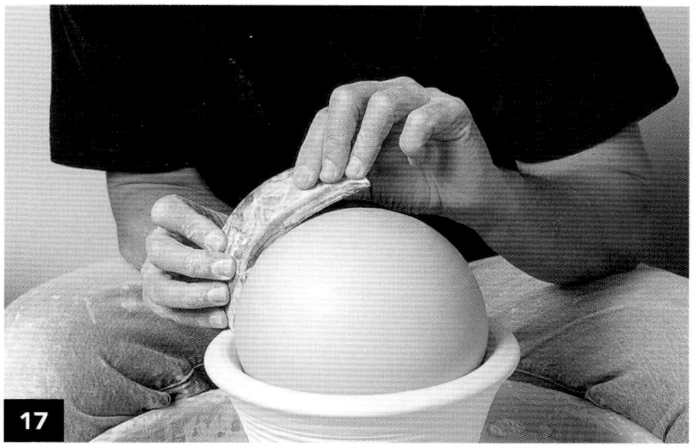

17

18

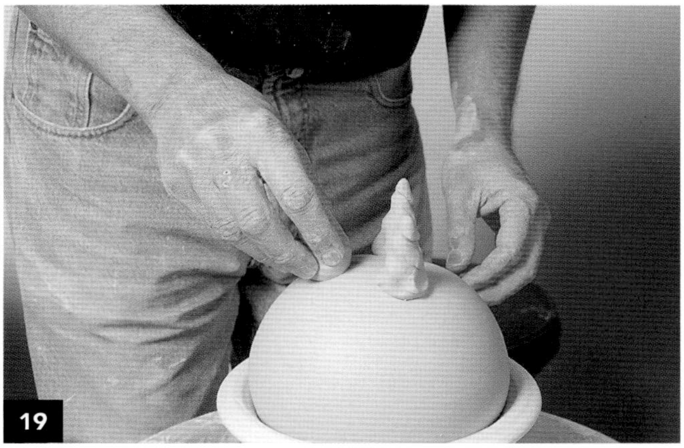

19

the liquid in the pot when the pot is full. Trace around the base of the spout with a needle tool or stick to mark its position; then set the spout back on the work surface. Now make some small holes within the traced area on the body in order to allow liquid to flow from the body into the spout. To help ensure an even flow of liquid, make sure that the total area of these holes exceeds that of the opening at the spout's tip. I use a fettling knife to make the holes, twisting and pushing it into the clay (Photo 20). Hollow tube hole makers also work well for this purpose.

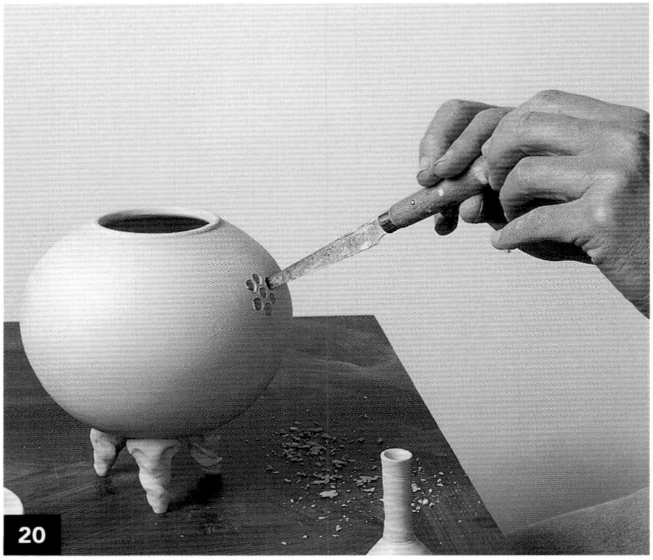

20

24. If you need to moisten the teapot's parts to keep them from drying out as you work, just spray them with water (Photo 21).

21

25. Before attaching the spout to the body, remove any excess clay from the inner surfaces at its base (Photo 22). Score the spout's base and the body, apply a bit of slurry to both, press the spout in

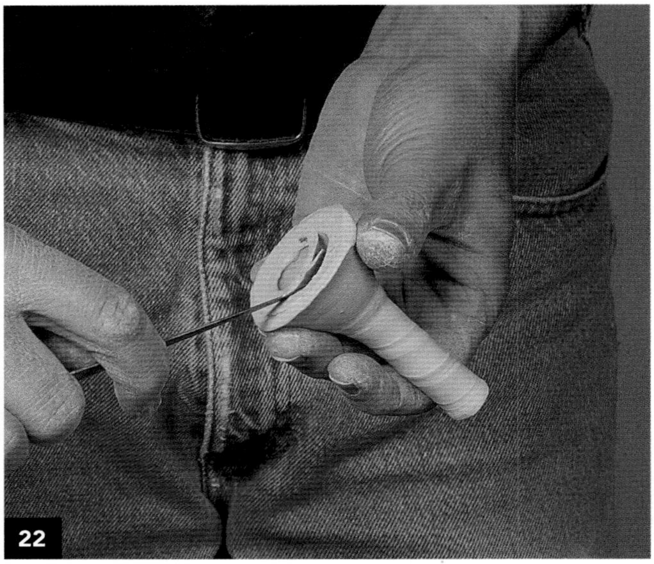

22

place, and use your fingertips to blend the clay at the joint (Photo 23). The spout should still be flexible enough to allow you to adjust its angle so that it successfully complements the pot.

23

26. I pull the handle on this teapot in the same way that I pull the handle on the pitcher (see pages 85-87). First, I attach a clay plug below the rim of the pot, opposite to the spout, making sure to leave enough space for the lid overhang. I then pull the handle, making it slightly longer than necessary so that I can pinch off any excess clay later. Next, I turn the pot upside down onto a board placed on a table, with the still moist handle hanging down past the edge of the table. When the handle has stiffened just enough to hold a shape, I turn the pot upright again, curve the handle to the desired shape, and cut away the excess clay from the free end (Photo 24).

24

25

Turning the teapot and soft handle right side up can be quite tricky. While the pot is still upside down, I loop the handle around to its near-final position and hold it in place with one hand. Then I grasp the pot and turn it over quickly, using my arms and whatever else works to help support the handle as I do. I have yet to find a graceful way to execute this maneuver; for the faint of heart, I'd suggest making another type of handle (see "Variations" at the end of this project).

27. Score and apply slurry to the free end of the handle and to the area just above the teapot spout where the handle and pot will be joined. To create a textured impression, I pressed the free end of this handle in place with a seashell instead of my fingertip (Photo 25). After pressing the handle in place, adjust its shape as necessary.

28. The assembled teapot must dry gradually, so cover it snugly with plastic for the first few days. (Loosen the covering towards the end of the drying period.) Fire pieces with added feet on a 1/4"-thick (6 mm) pancake of clay (or shrink pad) to avoid bending and cracking.

Variations

An alternative to rounding the bottom of the teapot and adding feet is to trim a foot ring on the bottom (see steps 9 to 14 on pages 60-61 for instructions). If the bottom of the form isn't too thick, you may want to trim only the outer edge of the foot, leaving a flat bottom on the pot. For your first teapots, either of these methods may be more appropriate than rounding the bottom and adding feet.

The handle technique described in this project is difficult to manage. Before attempting it, you may want to try one of the less frustrating alternatives that follow or one of the handle variations described on page 87.

Attaching a ready-made cane or homemade raffia handle like the one shown on the previous page is easy. Just make small loops of clay (or lugs), attach them to your teapot, and secure the handle to them after firing. These handles aren't as fragile as clay and can also be replaced when they begin to wear out.

Pull, coil, or extrude a smaller handle and add it to the side of the teapot opposite to the spout, just as pitcher handles are attached. This arrangement works well on many teapot forms, and the handles are less likely to be bumped or cracked during use than are handles looped over the top of the pot.

As you can see in the photo above, lids can vary widely. The one shown at the far left was thrown right side up; the others were thrown upside down. Notice the different ways in which they're seated on top of their forms. Except for the one on the left, these lids are also good for forms with wider openings, such as casseroles.

Spouts can also be made in a variety of ways. One method, for example, is to roll out a thin slab of clay and then wrap it around a wooden dowel. Spouts may also be pulled and hollowed, molded in a two-piece press mold, or extruded.

Possible Problems and Solutions

Problem: As you attempt the final shaping, the round body of the pot becomes too soft and is wobbly.

Solution: Set the pot aside to stiffen before continuing.

Problem: All your lids and spouts look awkward when you position them on the teapot body.

Solution: Keep the body moist by covering it tightly with plastic while you throw some more spouts and lids.

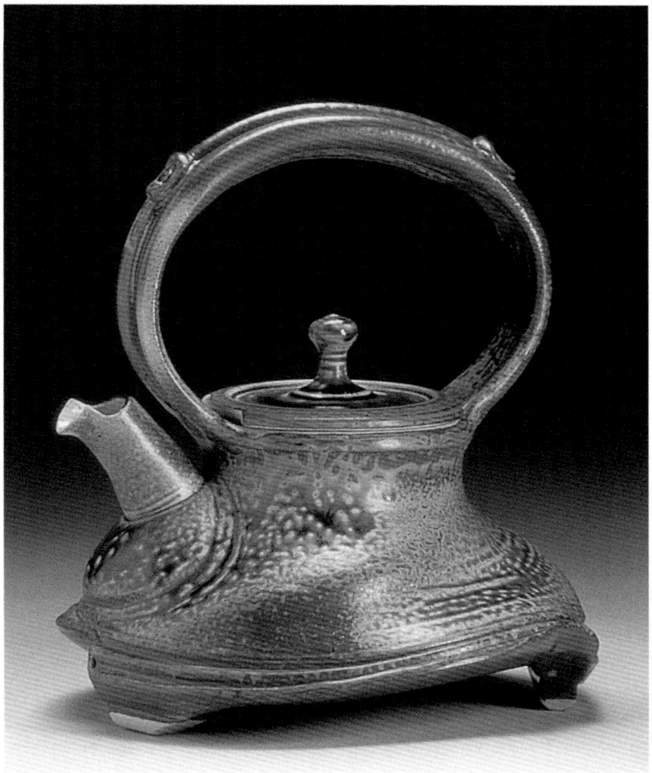

Top left: **Don Davis, *Teapot with Stand,*** 1993
Height: 22" (56 cm). Porcelain teapot thrown, with extruded and hand-built additions; bisque fired to cone 06; sprayed metallic colorant solutions, glaze trailed; interior glazed; glaze fired to cone 7, light reduction; earthenware stand hand-built and once fired to cone 1. Photo by Tim Barnwell

Top right: **Warren MacKenzie, *Tea Pot,*** 1995
8" x 7½" x 6" (20.5 x 19 x 15 cm). Stoneware; thrown, joined spout, beaten square, then cut; reduction fired in gas kiln to cone 10. Photo by Peter Lee

Right: **Charles Tefft, *Tea Pot,*** 1997
8" x 7¼" x 6¾" (20.5 x 18.5 x 17 cm). White stoneware; thrown, altered by pulling wooden tool up the inside while wet form turned on slowly spinning wheel, bottom paddled when leather hard, feet added, extruded handle with pulled ends; sprayed ash glazes; reduction fired in gas kiln to cone 10. Photo by Fabio Camara

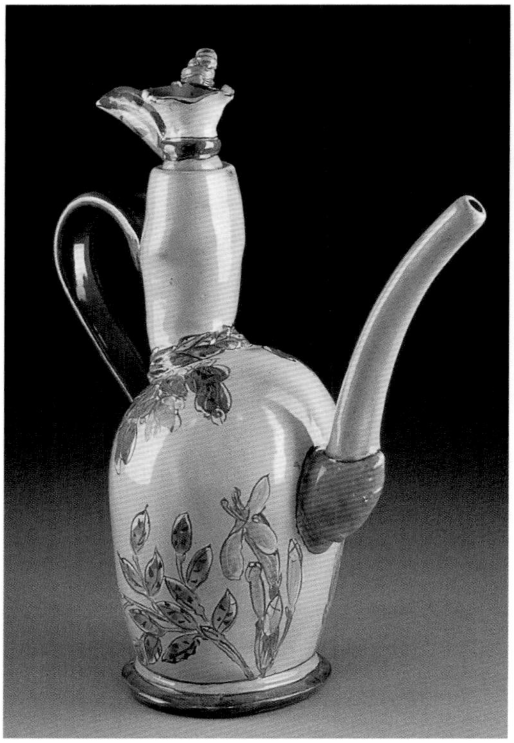

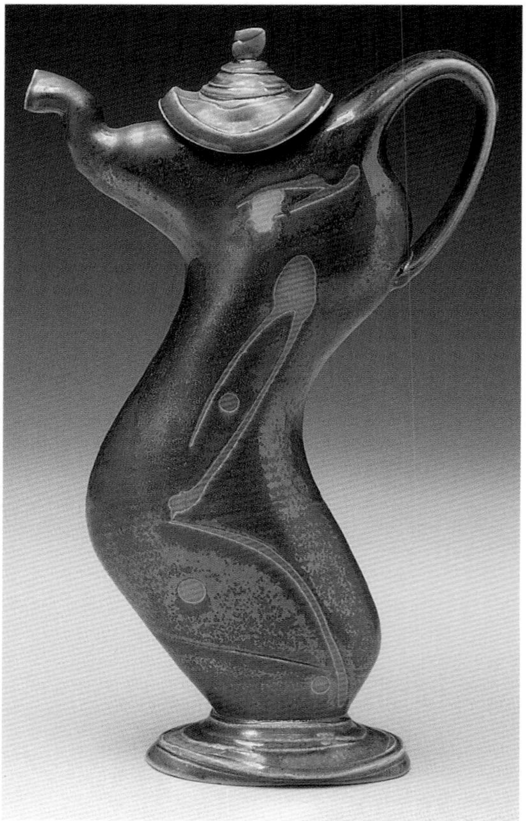

Top left: **Linda Arbuckle,** ***T-Pot: Shape of Spring,*** 1995
13" x 10" x 6" (33 x 25.5 x 15 cm). Terra-cotta; bottom thrown as closed form and made oval, top thrown and altered, spout pulled and hollowed; majolica glaze; oxidation fired in electric kiln to cone 03

Bottom left: **Marko Fields,** ***Smartass Teapot Thinks It's Alive; Oughta Join the Carnival,*** 1997
11" x 16" x 6" (28 x 40.5 x 15 cm). Porcelain, sterling silver, carnelian; base, smaller upper portion, stopper/lid, and spout lug all thrown and altered; pulled handle, slab-built top sections; handle, spout, and stopper incised; slabs press-molded; bisque fired; underglaze applied and wiped off; oxidation fired to cone 6; painted and sealed enamels. Photo by artist

Top right: **Shelley Schreiber,** ***Teapot,*** 1997
6½" x 9½" x 5" (16.5 x 24 x 12.5 cm). Porcelain; thrown; painted when leather hard with porcelain terra sigillata mixed with mason stain, then carved; bisque fired; dipped clear glaze; reduction fired in gas kiln to cone 10

Bottom right: **Nicholas Joerling,** ***Teapot,*** 1997
12" x 3" x 7" (30.5 x 7.5 x 18 cm). Stoneware; thrown, made oval, cut, and reassembled; thrown spout, lid, and foot added; handle pulled from pot; shino glaze, brushed wax resist, glazed again; fired to cone 10. Photo by Tim Barnwell

Right: **Posey Bacopoulos,** ***Square Teapot,*** 1997
7" x 8" x 6" (18 x 20.5 x 15 cm). Terra-cotta; body thrown and paddled square, collar and lid thrown separately, collar and feet attached, pulled handle; majolica glaze with colorants applied to glazed surface; fired in electric kiln to cone 04.
Photo by D. James Dee

Bottom left: **Walter Keeler,** ***Saltglazed Teapot,*** 1983
Height: 11" (28 cm). Stoneware. Photo courtesy of Garth Clark Gallery, New York, NY

Bottom right: **Diana Gillispie,** ***Teapot,*** 1993
9" x 4½" (23 x 11.5 cm). Red earthenware; thrown cylinder pressed into oval form, then attached to slab foot; handle and spout slab-built; majolica and stains; fired in electric kiln to cone 04.
Photo by Tim Barnwell

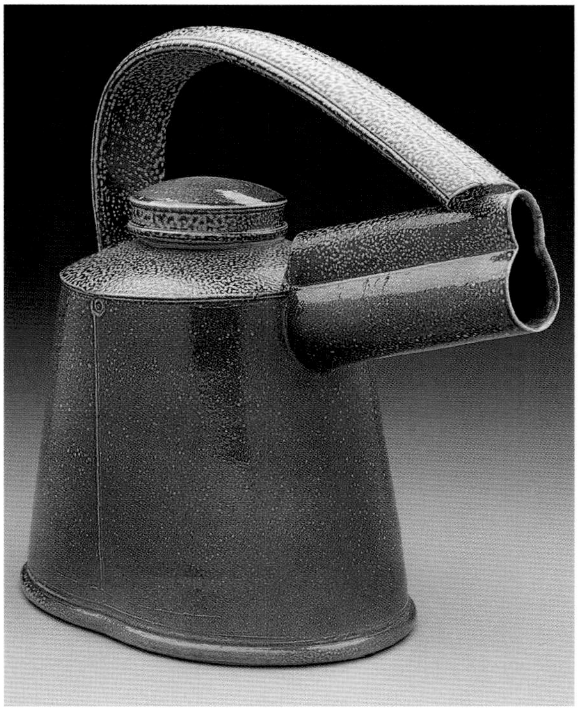

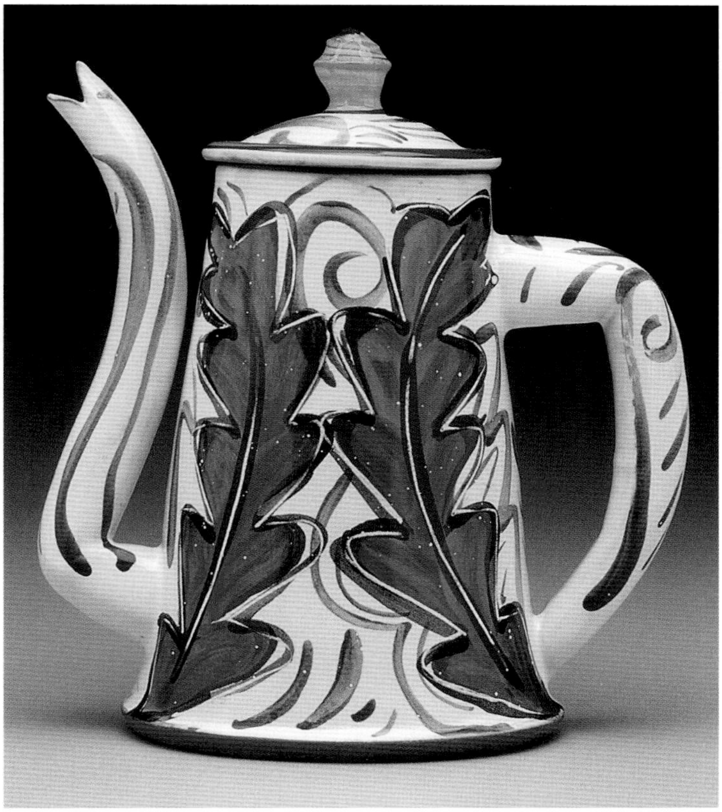

Elliptical Pot

Once you've mastered throwing round forms, you may want to try expanding a round shape into an elliptical one. Steven Forbes-deSoule demonstrates a special technique here, one that prevents gravity from collapsing the walls of his clay form as he stretches it wider and wider. As he expands the vessel, Steven stiffens both the upper shoulder and lower belly of the pot (the two areas most likely to collapse) by force-drying the clay in these areas with a propane torch and heat gun. Making the same vessel without force-drying the clay is possible, but the process takes much longer.

This pot requires at least 6 pounds (2.7 kg) of clay.

Starting Tips

■ The hotter your heat source, the thinner your clay walls, and the faster the wheel spins, the quicker the clay will dry when the heat is applied. Be patient with yourself! The more elliptical pots you throw, the better feel you'll have for how much heat to apply and how much you can stretch the clay without collapsing the form.

■ A propane torch is very hot indeed, so you must keep the flame moving continuously over the clay area to be dried. Exercise extreme caution using this tool: Never direct a torch towards your skin or anything flammable and be sure to turn it off when it's not in use. Steve recommends torches with automatic on/off switches and with flame spreaders on their tips.

■ Heat guns, usually used to strip paint from houses, come in various B.T.U. capacities. Although these tools aren't as hot as torches, they can still cause serious burns, so be careful. A hair dryer is the safest tool to use, but will take much longer to dry the clay.

■ Steve uses metal and rubber ribs to expand his vessels, but feel free to experiment with other tools or your hands. Exerting pressure with the tips of your fingers or a knuckle or thumb works well.

■ A mirror placed about 5 feet (1.5 m) away from your wheel will reflect the vessel's silhouette as you shape it and will help you keep track of the vessel's form (Photo 1).

1

Surface Treatment and Firing

Bisque fired to cone 06

Glazed with resist patterns

Raku fired to 1900°F (1038°C)

Instructions

1. Center the clay on the wheel and open it to create a flat bottom, about 2 to 3 inches (5 to 7.5 cm) in diameter and ¼ inch (6 mm) thick. This portion of the clay will constitute the final foot of your vessel, but as you shape the clay walls in subsequent steps, you'll need a thicker, wider base than this foot provides in order to support the clay as you work. To create this temporary working base, which you'll trim away later, continue to open the clay back another 2 to 3 inches, raising your hands slightly so that the outer portion of the flat base will be thicker than the inner portion.

2. Pull the walls up several times to form a slightly conical shape with straight sides and a narrow lip opening (Photo 2). The bottom wall should be

2

between ½ and ¾ inch (1.3 to 1.9 cm) thick, and the neck should be at least ⅜ inch (1 cm) thick. (A neck that's too thin will make the shape more prone to collapse.)

3. Next, you must pull the form into a round shape. With each pull, start by expanding the bottom wall, exerting outward pressure with the hand inside the vessel and supporting the clay with the hand outside the vessel. As your hands rise above the widest portion of the vessel, your outer hand will rise slightly above your inside hand and the inward pressure it provides will keep the neck from drifting outward. Keep the neck opening narrow and, for added strength, establish an upward curve between the shoulder and lip.

4. As you continue pulling, use a metal or wooden rib on the outside of the form to compress and smooth the surface (Photo 3). This will remove the throwing rings and will strengthen the piece. At this point, use a wooden stick to trim away any excess clay from the base.

3

5. Using a sponge and then a flexible rubber rib, remove all the slurry from the inside bottom of the piece. Then, gently use the rubber rib to remove any slurry from the inside belly, shoulder, and neck areas.

6. With the wheel spinning, begin applying heat to the shoulder and lower belly areas. The trick is to dry the belly and shoulder evenly while avoiding overdrying. As you can see in Photo 4, Steve uses

4

a propane torch and heat gun simultaneously. He props the heat gun on a bed of clay, directing its nozzle towards the lower belly of the pot. This leaves his hands free to aim the torch towards the pot's shoulder.

Use the torch to heat the shoulder for about 1½ to 2 minutes. To ensure even drying, keep the torch moving and the wheel spinning. If you see any steam escaping from the clay, remove the torch immediately. The heat gun, which will take longer to dry the clay, should stay on for 5 to 6 minutes. If you're working without a heat gun, use the torch to dry the lower belly as well, applying heat for 2 or 3 minutes or until the desired dryness is achieved.

7. Turn off both heat sources. With the wheel turning, begin pushing the lower belly outward, using a rubber rib on the inside of the pot to provide outward pressure and a flexible rubber or metal rib to compress the outer surface (Photo 5).

5

Gently release the pressure when the clay at the lower belly has expanded by about 1 inch (2.5 cm) in diameter. Gradual stretching is the key.

8. Change your grip on the rubber rib as shown in Photo 7, and repeat step 7 at the shoulder of the piece (Photo 6). Increase the shoulder diameter by no more than 1 inch.

9. Expand the belly area by pushing the clay out gently, using the rubber rib on the inside and the metal rib on the outside (Photo 7).

10. If you're using a torch, reapply heat for no more than 15 to 20 seconds before continuing. (A heat gun will take somewhat longer.) Now repeat steps

6

7

7 and 8 several times, expanding the vessel gradually (Photos 8 and 9). As you do this, you may need to further stiffen the lower belly and shoulder somewhat. Keep in mind that the more elliptical your vessel becomes, the slower the wheel should be turning.

11. When the body of the vessel is stretched to the desired shape, apply slurry to the outside and inside of the neck. Then, with the wheel turning, push the neck in so the opening is approximately the same diameter as the desired bottom of the piece (Photo 10). Finish the lip as desired.

12. Set the vessel aside to dry until the shoulder and neck are leather hard. In the piece of foam rubber, cut a hole just large enough to accommodate the vessel's neck. Then flip the vessel over, set the neck into the hole, and allow the bottom of the vessel to dry to leather hard. To prevent uneven drying, avoid drafts.

13. Place the vessel upside down on the greenware chuck. Using a torpedo level, check the bottom to make sure it will stay even when the piece

8

9

10

turns on the wheel (Photo 11). Then, while stopping and starting the wheel, center the base of the vessel on the bat by gently pushing on the side of the chuck.

14. To trim away the excess clay from the foot, first use a loop trimming tool to mark the desired foot diameter on the clay (Photo 12). This diameter should match the 2- to 3-inch-diameter base you established in step 2. Then remove the excess clay. (Let the shape of the belly guide you as you shape the contour of the foot.)

11

12

15. Finish the bottom as desired (Photo 13). Allow the vessel to dry upside down on the piece of foam rubber for several hours before flipping it over. This will help prevent sagging of the thin lower belly walls.

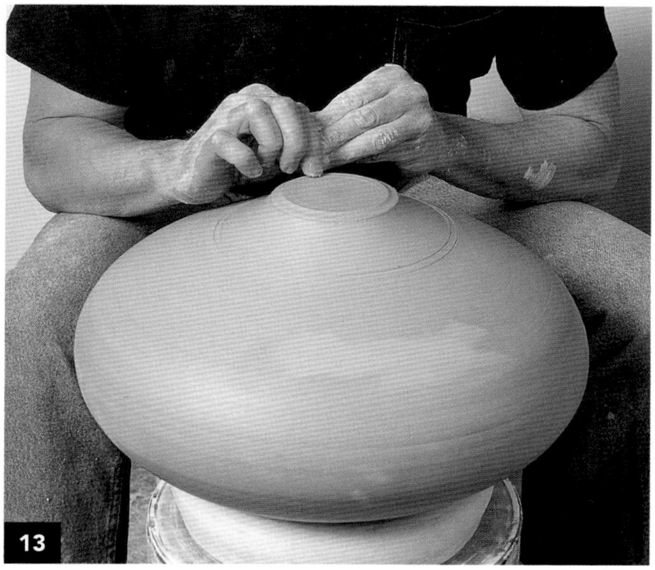

13

Top left: **Jose Ortiz, *Serenata,*** 1997
27" x 18" x 18" (68.5 x 45.5 x 45.5 cm). Thrown in four parts and assembled; oxides and incising; wood fired to cone 08; acrylics. Photo by Peter Chartrand

Top right: **Karen Koblitz, *Santa Caterina of Deruta,*** 1997
24¾" x 8½" x 8½" (63 x 21.5 x 21.5 cm). Low-fire white clay; vase and base thrown, the vase in three sections; carved; bisque fired to cone 04; underglazes and glazes fired to cone 06; lusters fired to cone 017. Photo by Susan Einstein

Left: **Steven Forbes-deSoule, *Ballard Harvest Moon,*** 1997
12" x 15" x 15" (30.5 x 38 x 38 cm). Raku; thrown and trimmed body and lid; glazes applied with wax resist; raku fired to cone 06; acrylics airbrushed in unglazed areas; lid embellished with paua shell

Top left: **Helio Gutierrez,** ***Maraca,*** 1997
10½" x 8" x 8" (26.5 x 20.5 x 20.5 cm). Thrown in one piece, incised when leather hard; oxides applied to greenware, then burnished; wood fired once to cone 08; acrylics rubbed in after firing.
Photo by Peter Chartrand

Top right: **Carl Baker,** ***Brushwork Vase,*** 1996
15" x 15" x 15" (38 x 38 x 38 cm). White stoneware/porcelain; thrown and ribbed; brushed slips on bisque-fired ware; clear glaze over slip; fired, heavy reduction, in gas kiln, to cone 6.
Photo by George Post Photo

Right: **Ben Owen III,** ***Lily Jar—Chinese Red,*** 1997
12½" x 8½" x 8½" (32 x 21.5 x 21.5 cm). Earthenware; thrown; fired in electric kiln to cone 07. Photo by David Ramsey

HEART-SHAPED VASE

This vase form is inspired by traditional European and North American stoneware storage vessels. The strength and feeling of fullness that those vessels project endures through time. For my own contemporary interpretation, I have narrowed the base and extended the neck to create a little more visual tension in the shape.

As you begin to work with larger amounts of clay in order to make larger pieces, you'll need to adjust your throwing technique. The larger the piece, the more force and control are required to form the clay. As potters work upward in scale, it sometimes becomes obvious that "big" is not necessarily "good." Everything is magnified when you work with larger forms, including any flaws. Working on a large scale, however, can be a rewarding challenge, and when it's done well, some wonderful results can occur. "Large" is a relative term, of course, and will hold different meanings for each individual.

The best way to achieve confidence with larger forms is to gradually increase the amount of clay that you work with. When you're comfortable throwing 2 pounds (.9 kg) of clay, try using 4 pounds (1.8 kg), and when you're comfortable with 4 pounds, try 5 (2.3 kg), then 6 (2.7 kg), and so on. When you reach a comfortable limit, you may want to add sections instead of struggling with ever larger pieces of clay. With some forms, even though they're not large, it's simply more convenient to add on a section than to make the entire piece out of one lump of clay.

I threw the bottom section of this vase with 10 pounds (4.5 kg) of clay and the top section with 2 pounds (.9 kg). Making a smaller piece of the same shape with one lump of clay would be possible, but the "adding-on" technique demonstrated in this project becomes necessary when you're working on a piece as large as the one shown.

Surface Treatment and Firing

Bisque fired to cone 06

Interior glazed; exterior trailed with glaze and sprayed with stains over tape resist, tape removed, sprayed again, brushwork in resist area with oxide solution

Glaze fired to cone 7, light reduction in gas-fired kiln

Instructions

1. After throwing and finalizing the shape of the bottom section, leave it in place on the bat and remove the bat from the wheel. (If you have to cut it loose with your wire, remember to use four large plugs of clay to hold it in place when you return it to the wheel to add the top section.) Let the thrown form dry until the clay is medium leather

hard. It should be stiff enough to support the clay you'll be adding on, but still soft enough to be a little flexible. If the bottom section becomes too dry, some cracking will occur after the top is added and has started to dry.

Monitoring the bottom section carefully as it dries is critical. Uneven drying and the resulting warpage can make throwing the top section in place impossible. To speed up the drying process, I sometimes use a torch and have even dropped burning bits of crumpled paper inside the form. My favorite method, however, is to let the bottom section air-dry more slowly. As with most of my pieces, I throw several in a day. As they sit on their bats, I rotate them one-quarter turn every 20 minutes or so to ensure even drying. (You may need to cover the upper portion to slow down its drying so the lower portion can catch up.)

2. When the bottom section is ready, measure its opening with calipers. Then throw a collar of clay on another bat, but don't cut it off. Open the collar all the way down to the bat and make it large enough at its top to fit on the rim of the opening in the bottom section.

3. Place the bottom section and its bat back on the wheel, make sure the piece is centered, and score and moisten its rim. Then turn the bat with the collar on it upside down and place the collar evenly on top of the rim of the bottom section (Photo 1). Use a cutoff wire to separate the collar from the bat; then remove the bat.

1

4. With the wheel turning quite slowly, use your fingers, both inside and outside to push the top section onto the rim of the bottom section (Photo 2). Because the wall of the collar is thicker than that of the rim, the collar will overlap both the inner and outer surfaces of the rim. Your wheel must turn slowly so you won't knock the pot off the bat as you work on the top section.

2

5. Pull and shape the top section. Throwing an added section requires delicate fingertip control. You must raise the clay gingerly, without creating too much upward drag. I left a thick rim to strengthen and emphasize the top of this vessel (Photo 3).

3

6. With the wheel turning slowly, draw a cutting stick down the exterior wall of the piece to remove any

excess clay at the base (Photo 4). As the wheel continues to turn, hold the tip of the cutting stick just above the cut and trickle water down it (Photo 5). (This water-trickling technique will be most useful on a moist piece, right after throwing.) Then use the cutting tool to cut the ring loose from the bat (Photo 6). Bevel the base with the stick before releasing the pot

from the bat. When the upper portion is leather hard, cover the piece with plastic for a few days to prevent cracking as it dries.

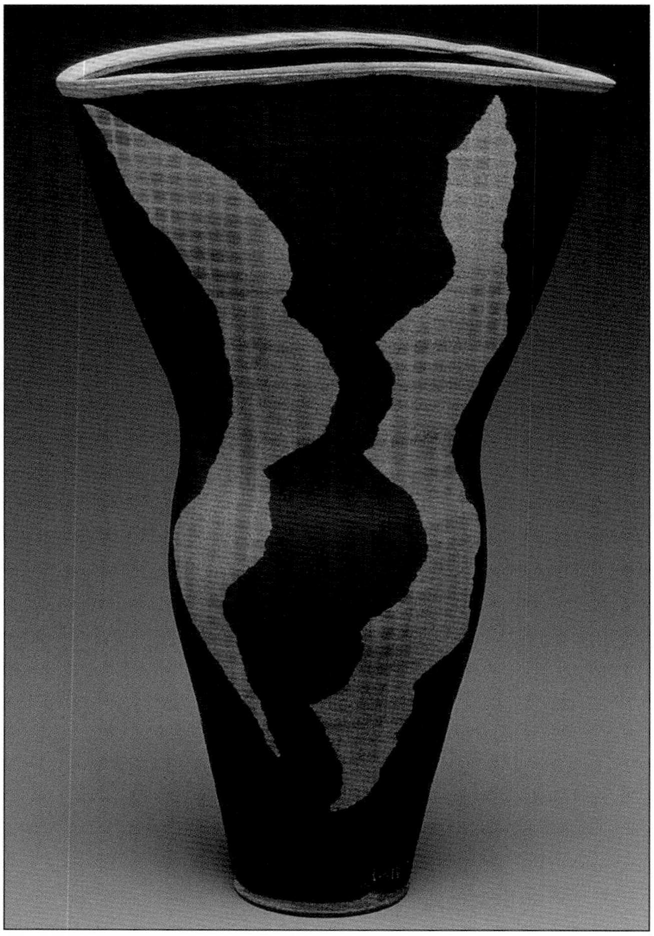

Variations

The adding-on technique can be used to achieve a wide variety of forms. A traditional variation on this technique is the addition of a series of thick coils to a leather-hard bottom section. A few coils are added, thrown, and then allowed to stiffen before more are added. With this method, the size of your kiln is the only limit to the size of the piece you make.

The vase shown in the photo above was inspired by ancient Japanese Jomon ware. Although Jomon vessels were hand-built, the tremendous strength inherent in their flowing forms speaks to the thrower. And although they were made 5,000 years ago by a culture about which we know very little, these great works are timeless. As with many of my forms, the original inspiration serves as a solid starting place for me. Using these inspirations, I let my own experience guide the forms I make. This one suggests the form of a human torso.

The torso vase differs from the heart-shaped vase in that after the top section is added to and pulled on the bottom section, the two sections are shaped together as one continuous form. The added section is blended and ribbed, so that no obvious line or break in the form occurs at the joint.

I start by throwing the cylindrical bottom section, with its very slight outward curve, using about 10 pounds (4.5 kg) of clay. After this section is leather hard, I pull the top section once, and then add it to the bottom section, just as I added the top section to the heart-shaped vase (Photo 7). The top section requires 7 pounds (3.2 kg) of clay.

7

Next, I pull the added section to its maximum height (Photo 8). Then I rib and blend the sections, shaping them together to create a continuous contour (Photo 9). I shaped this vessel outward to imply hips, necked it in a bit to indicate the torso's waist, and flared it out toward the top to suggest shoulders.

After the top section stiffens, I gradually push the piece into an oval and dent it vertically down the middle. Pushing a vase into an oval changes its appearance dramatically. Suddenly, it has a front, back, and sides. When the altering has been completed and the top is leather hard, I cover the entire piece tightly with plastic for a few days before allowing it to dry.

8

9

Possible Problems and Solutions

Problem: The upper portion of the bottom section is off center when you place it back on the wheel. Sometimes the pot will lean to one side because it was bumped when you moved it.

Solution: Push the leather-hard clay carefully back into position.

Problem: The bottom section pops loose while you're trying to pull or shape the top.

Solution: Catch it quickly! If the piece isn't damaged, recenter it, and hold it in place by pressing four lumps of clay around it, onto the bat, as you do when trimming a foot (see page 60). Your wheel may have been spinning too quickly, so slow it down before continuing.

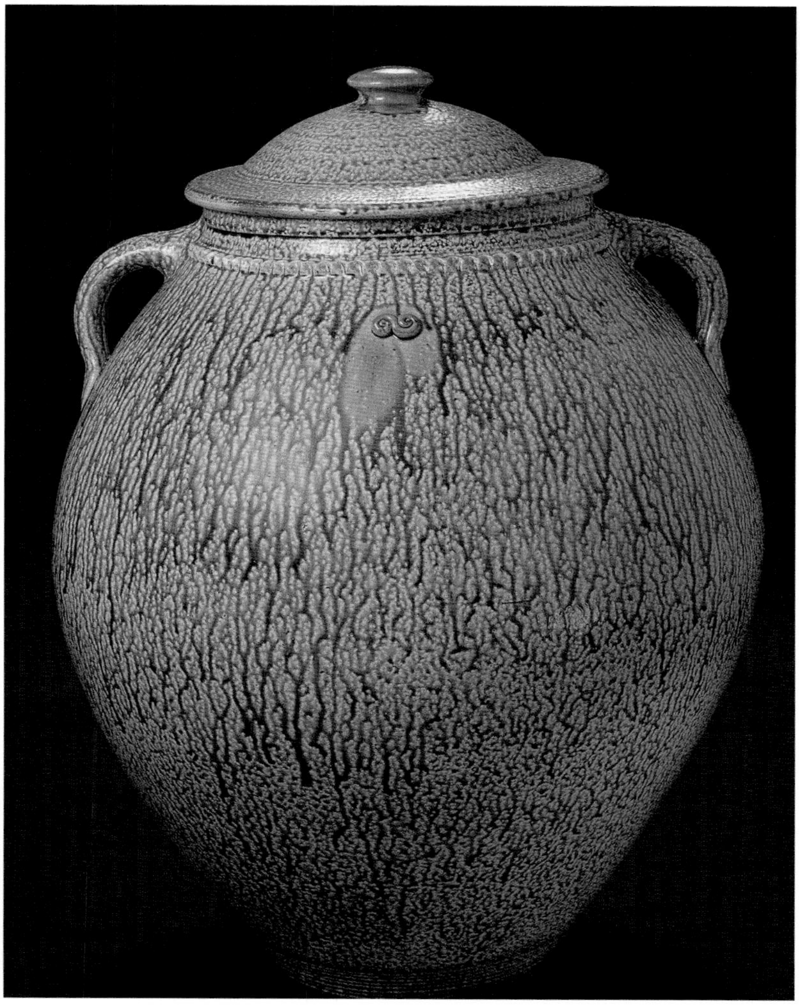

Top left: **Coll Minogue,** ***Lidded Jar,*** 1997
5½" x 5½" x 5½" (14 x 14 x 14 cm). Stoneware; thrown, coiled knob; incised lines and impressed stamping; once fired for 24 hours in Bourry box wood-fired kiln to cone 11. Photo by Paul Adair

Top right: **Don McCance,** ***Sterility Figure,*** 1997
24" x 16" x 16" (61 x 40.5 x 40.5 cm). Red earthenware; thrown bottom with hand-built figure; glaze, engobes, sprigging; glaze fired in electric kiln to cone 04-06

Left: **Mark Hewitt,** ***Large Covered Jar,*** 1995
Height: 36" (91.5 cm). Stoneware; thrown and coiled sections; wood-fired to cone 12; salted ash glaze with blue glass runs

Top left: **Sandy Vitarelli,** ***Harvest,*** 1990
36" x 18" x 18" (91.5 x 45.5 x 45.5 cm). Stoneware; thrown in sections; Maui earth slip applied, sgraffito; once fired, reduction, to cone 8. Photo by artist

Top right: **Ken Ferguson,** ***Parade Pot,*** 1990
Height: 14½" x 17" (37 x 43 cm). Black stoneware; chrome slip.
Photo by E.G. Schempf, courtesy of Garth Clark Gallery, New York, NY

Right: **Josh DeWeese,** ***Jar,*** 1997
16" x 13" x 13" (40.5 x 33 x 33 cm). Stoneware; thrown and trimmed; flashing slip applied to bone-dry ware; five-day anagama wood firing to cone 12, with pot laid on its side in oyster shells. Photo by artist

Left: **David Regan, *Tureen,*** 1993
Height: 18" (45.5 cm). Porcelain; sgraffito; salt glazed. Photo courtesy of Garth Clark Gallery, New York, NY

Bottom left: **Val Cushing, *Covered Jar ("Acorn" series),*** 1990
Height: 26" (66 cm). Thrown in one piece; reduction fired

Bottom right: **Burlon Craig, *Jug,*** circa 1980
11" x 6½" x 6½" (28 x 16.5 x 16.5 cm). Traditional Catawba Valley alkaline-glazed stoneware, locally dug clay; snake and pulled handle added; wood fired in groundhog kiln. Collection of Don Davis; photo by Evan Bracken

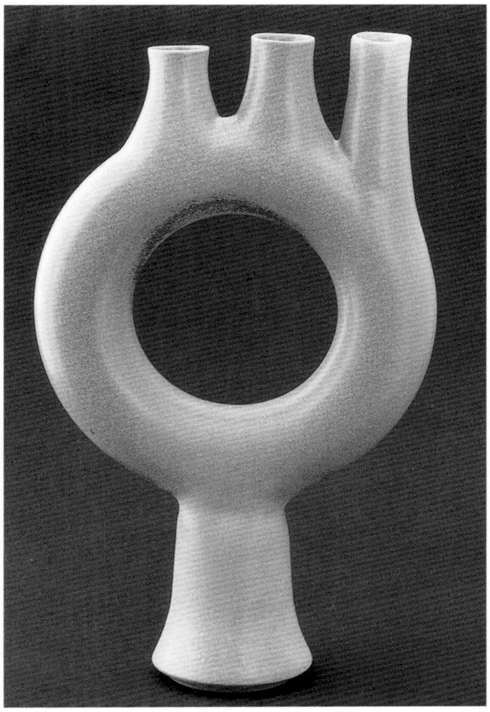

Top left: **Sid Oakley and John Martin,** ***Crystalline Porcelain,*** 1994
1" x 4" x 4" (2.5 x 10 x 10 cm). Thrown; crystalline glaze; oxidation fired in electric kiln to cone 11. Photo by Seth Tice-Lewis; collection of Will Tucker

Top center: **Audry Yoder Heatwole,** ***Thrice Intercepted,*** 1989
17" x 7" x 2" (43 x 18 x 5 cm). Porcelain; thrown in five parts and assembled when leather hard; sprayed glaze; reduction fired (very light) in gas kiln to cone 9

Top right: **Julie Olson,** ***Spirit Vessel,*** 1997
8" x 4" x 4" (20.5 x 10 x 10 cm). Raku; thrown and carved, feet cut from base with a wire; raku fired to cone 04.
Photo by Pete Cozart

Right: **Robert Moore,** ***Tureen,*** 1997
22" x 18" x 15" (56 x 45.5 x 38 cm). White stoneware; thrown parts altered with fingers and assembled; copper-bearing glaze; salt fired, light reduction, to cone 10. Photo by Boomer

Creamers and Sauceboats

Sauces, creams, and gravies are generally served in boat-shaped vessels. These usually have pouring lips or spouts, handles, and—sometimes—lids. Leah Leitson, who demonstrates this project, uses a technique that makes it possible to create forms difficult to achieve in any other way. As you'll see, this piece is thrown upside down. Leah's method includes throwing the body of the vessel upside down, without a bottom, by opening the clay right down to the bat and then closing off the top.

You'll need ¾ to 1 pound (.3 to .5 kg) of clay to make this vessel. Leah uses porcelain.

Surface Treatment and Firing

Bisque fired to cone 06
Dipped in transparent glaze
Glaze fired (oxidation) to cone 6

Instructions

1. Center the clay on the wheel. Then open the clay to the bat. The inside diameter should be 5 inches (12.7 cm).
2. Pull the walls to the desired height, tapering the clay inward at the rim (Photo 1).
3. Gradually collar in the opening by narrowing the neck until it closes (Photo 2).
4. Using a flexible metal rib, complete the shaping of the form (Photo 3).
5. To create the undulating lobes, turn the wheel slowly and draw a wooden rib up the form in three or four locations, pressing inward and upward as you do (Photo 4). The air trapped inside will make the closed form amazingly resistant and springy and will allow you to press on the walls without collapsing the clay. To soften these lines, wipe them with a damp sponge.

6. Use a cutoff wire to separate the form from the bat. Then place the form on a board and allow it to dry until the clay is medium leather hard.

2

3

4

7. To make the foot, first throw a small, doughnut-shaped ring off the hump. (See pages 102-103 for details.)

8. When the form is leather hard, place it back on the wheel and secure it to the bat by pressing lumps of moist clay around it.

9. Score and apply slip to the surface of the form, where you plan to attach the foot. Then place the doughnut-shaped moist clay ring onto the form (Photo 5). Press the ring securely in place, smoothing the moist clay to fasten it securely.

5

10. To shape the ring into a foot, pull its walls upward and outward (Photo 6).

6

11. Remove the bat from the wheel, leaving the form in place and uncovered until the foot has

stiffened enough to support the form when the piece is turned right side up. This will probably take several hours. As the foot dries, you'll need to dip the rim in water once or twice to keep it soft enough to manipulate.

12. When the foot is leather hard, you'll need to shape the pouring lip. First use your thumb and index finger to thin the clay wall by squeezing and pinching it. Then pull it outward and away from the form (Photo 7). To prevent your creamer or sauceboat from pouring too quickly or dripping, make sure the lip you pull is thin and almost sharp edged.

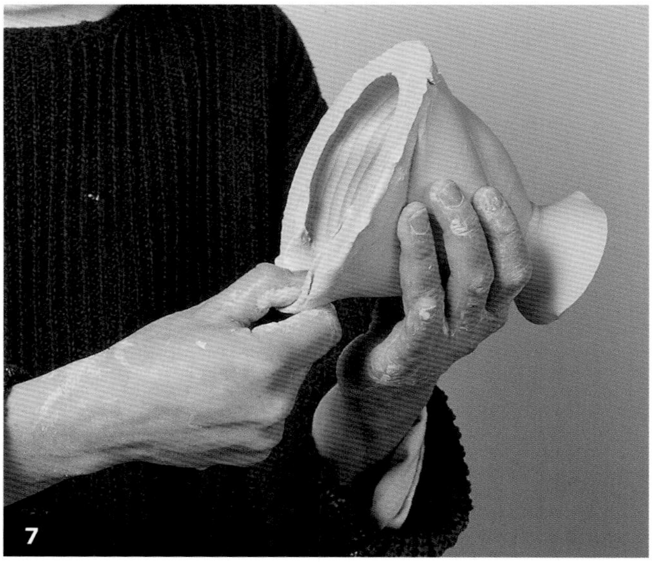
7

13. When the rim of the piece is leather hard, shape it by cutting the clay (Photo 8). You may want to sketch a cutting line first with a needle tool. If the rim has stiffened too much to cut easily, just mist it with water, moisten it with a damp sponge, or wrap it in damp newspaper and let it sit for awhile.

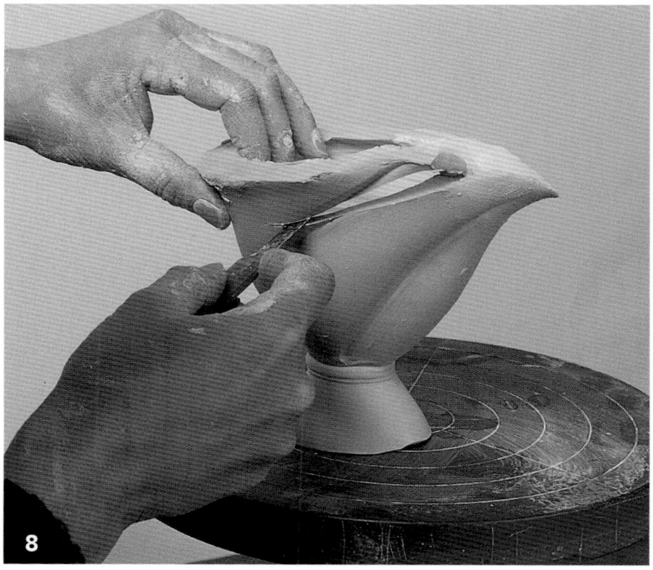
8

14. After shaping the rim, use a damp sponge to soften the cut edges (Photo 9). To enhance the lobes in the form, manipulate the rim in or out as desired.

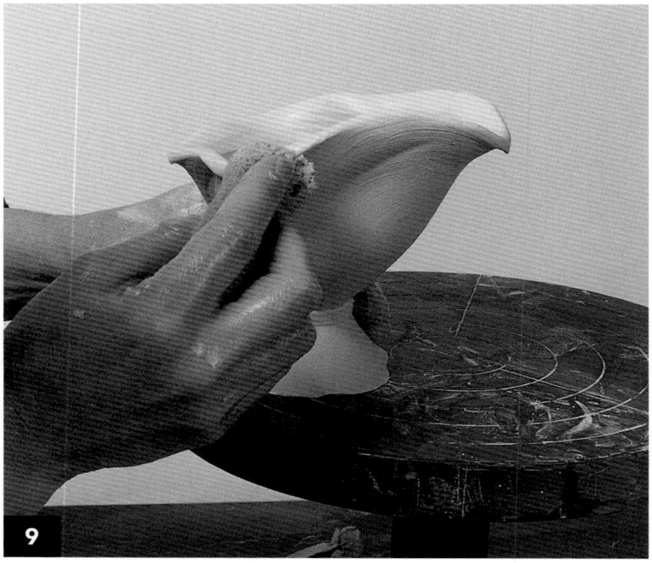
9

15. Leah pulls her creamer and sauceboat handles directly from the thrown and altered bodies so that they look as if they were growing right from the forms themselves. Start by following the instructions on pages 85-86 to pull an incomplete handle.

16. Using a ruler, make a notch in the fat end of the handle (Photo 10).

10

17. Fit the notch over the rim (Photo 11). To secure the handle in place, smooth the moist clay onto the inner and outer surfaces of the body.

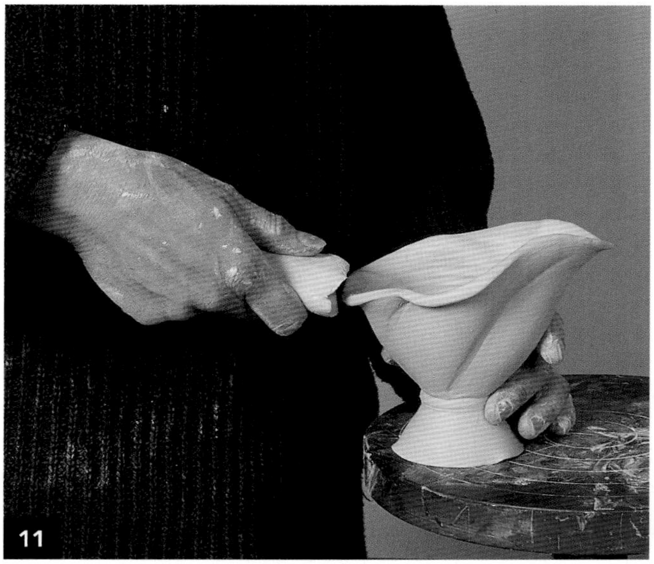
11

18. Using Photo 12 as a guide, hold the body in one hand and finish pulling the handle with the other. As you can see in this photo, the appearance of Leah's vessel is enhanced by the throwing rings on its inner surface.

12

19. Cut the handle to the desired length and secure the free end in place just above the foot (Photo 13). When the handle is leather hard, Leah adds a small coil of moist clay between the bottom of the handle and the body wall just above it, pressing and smoothing the coil to fill the small, V-shaped space. She does this in order to make the handle appear as if it were flowing back into the vessel.

13

Top: **Bonnie Seeman,** ***Tremona,*** 1997
12" x 18" x 18" (30.5 x 45.5 x 45.5 cm).
Porcelain; pitcher body thrown as round form, squeezed into oval, grooved; spout cut from thrown cylinder; tray thrown as bowl, stretched, and altered while wet; carved, drawn on; oxidation bisque fired to cone 10; china painted; multiple firings to cone 018

Right: **Mary Tyson Bertmaring,** ***"Ollie"® (olive oil vessel) and Guppy (espresso pot),*** 1997
Oil vessel: 6" x 4" x 2" (15 x 10 x 5 cm).
Porcelain; oil vessel body and spout thrown and altered, with slab-built bottom and hand-built stopper; espresso pot body slip-cast, with thrown lid and foot, hand-built handle; slip and sgraffito; bisque fired in electric kiln; fired in gas kiln to cone 11. Photo by Diane Davis

Top: **Leah Leitson,** ***Cruet Set,*** 1997
Tray: 1" x 4" x 10½" (2.5 x 10 x 26.5 cm). Porcelain; thrown and altered; fired in electric kiln to cone 5. Photo by Tim Barnwell

Center left: **W.B. Stephen (1876-1961),** ***Cameo Coffee Pot,*** Pisgah Forest Pottery, 1937
Height: 12" (30.5 cm). The cameo design was achieved by painting layers of liquid clay onto the form, allowing each layer to dry before applying the next. Photo courtesy of Sid Oakley and the Museum of American Pottery

Right: **Kreg Richard Owens,** ***Cream & Sugar Stack,*** 1996
14" x 5" x 5" (35.5 x 12.5 x 12.5 cm). Terra-cotta; both thrown as closed cones; sugar inverted when leather hard, opening cut, and top faceted, hand-built base, legs, and lugs attached; creamer trimmed to remove bottom, rolled when leather hard on textured canvas, stamped, and attached to thrown, textured, altered slab base; hand-built feet, coiled opening, inset lid, pulled handle, thrown spout, hand-built finials; terra sigillata exteriors, glazed interiors; once fired, oxidation, to cone 04

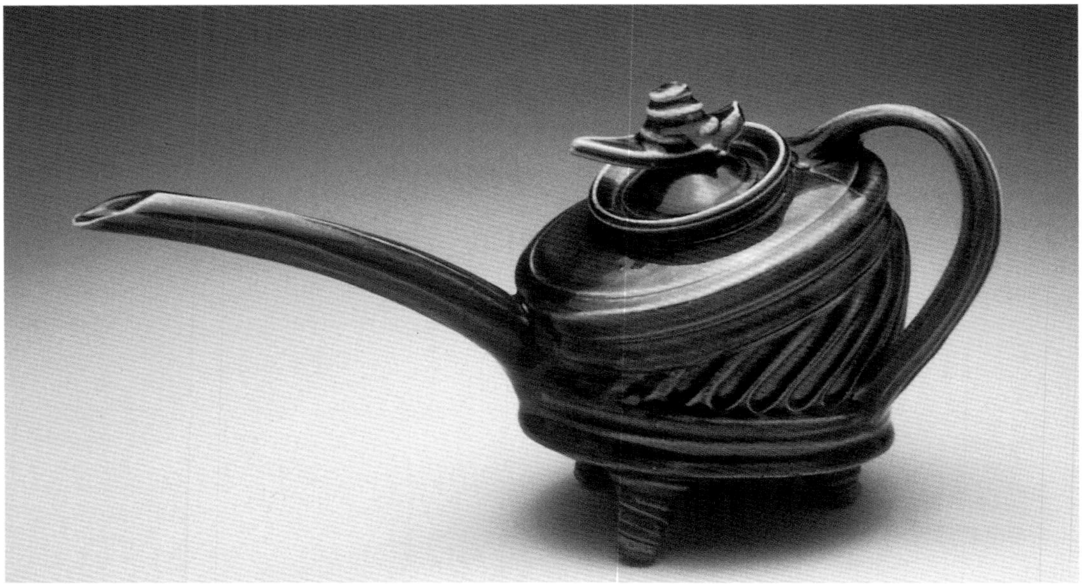

Top: **John F. Byrd,** ***Gas Can,*** 1997
8" x 12" x 5" (20.5 x 30.5 x 12.5 cm). Red earthenware; made with thrown cylinder shaped into oval and thrown, cut, and folded slabs; layered slips; soda fired to cone 04. Photo by artist

Center: **Gerry Dinnen,** ***Dojō Warrior,*** 1994
5" x 5" x 12" (12.5 x 12.5 x 30.5 cm). Stoneware; body thrown, cut, fluted, reattached, and slab constructed; feet thrown, handles thrown and hand-built, spout pulled; sprayed glaze; salt fired to cone 10. Photo by artist

Left: **Silvie Granatelli,** ***Soy/Oil Bottle,*** 1997
4" x 4" x 3" (10 x 10 x 7.5 cm). Porcelain; thrown without bottom, altered, spouts attached at leather-hard stage, incised; dipped glaze; fired in gas kiln to cone 10. Photo by Tim Barnwell

Top left: **Chris Staley,** ***Untitled,*** 1988
Height: 18" (45.5 cm). Black stoneware. Photo courtesy of Garth Clark Gallery, New York, NY

Top right: **Ole Morten Rokvam,** ***6303,*** 1997
18" x 11" x 19" (45.5 x 28 x 48.5 cm). White stoneware; thrown and trimmed parts, plus hand-built parts; assembled; glazed; reduction fired to cone 10; sandblasted

Right: **Laurie Rolland,** ***Cream and Sugar,*** 1997
Creamer: 7" x 6¼" x 3" (18 x 16 x 7.5 cm). Stoneware; creamer base thrown, body hand-built; sugar thrown in two pieces, upper portion drape molded, lid thrown; slip glazes and stains; electric kiln fired to cone 6. Photo by artist

Double-Walled Bowl

Norm Schulman was introduced to double-walled pots in 1950, when he found a fourteenth or fifteenth century Persian pitcher in the collection of the Metropolitan Museum of Art in New York City. The outer wall of the pitcher was reticulated—carved with flowing, stylized vines and leaves. At that time, Norm had been giving a great deal of thought to the duality of man's nature and the dualities manifested by individuals. To him, the double-walled form of the Persian pitcher was a meaningful metaphor for these dualities, and the concept of expressing duality through his own vessels took shape.

The double-walled vessel forms he imagined and later made were architectonic, with occasional departures into rough organic expressions. Norm worked on this principle, abandoned it for 20 years, and has since returned to try it from a different perspective. The bowl that he presents here requires 10 to 15 pounds (4.5 to 6.8 kg) of clay.

Surface Treatment and Firing

Painted with terra sigillata when bone dry
Fired (oxidation) to cone 3

Instructions

1. Center the clay on the wheel.
2. Open the clay all the way down to the surface of the bat, moving it outward to form a solid ring (Photos 1 and 2). The inner portion of this ring will form the interior wall of the bowl; the outer portion will form the exterior wall.
3. Using a wooden rib, scrape away any excess clay that remains on the bat inside the ring (Photo 3).
4. To form the two walls, you must split the ring down its center. While the wheel turns, shape a groove in the center of the ring by pressing down firmly with one finger (Photo 4). As you do this, support the inner and outer walls with your hands. When you're finished, the clay at the base of the groove should

1

2

3

4

be ¼- to ⅜-inch (6 to 10 mm) thick and should connect the two clay walls on either side of it.

5. Being careful not to disturb the outer ring, begin pulling the interior ring as you would a closed form, to make an upside-down bowl (Photo 5). As you can see in Photo 6, Norm uses a rib to remove excess clay and smooth the inner surface of the bowl as he works.

5

6

6. After closing the neck to form the bowl (Photos 7 and 8), use a flexible metal rib to smooth the bowl's outer surface (Photo 9).

7

8

9

7. Pull the outer ring to shape the foot (or outer wall) of the bowl (Photo 10). Make sure this foot ring is strong and true.

10

8. Use a flexible metal rib again to smooth the outer surface of the foot (Photo 11). If you were to slice your double-walled bowl in half at this stage, it would look very much like the half-bowl shown in Photo 12.

11

12

9. Using a cutoff wire, separate the bowl form from the bat. (The texture of the wire you use—twisted or smooth—will determine the texture and character of your bowl's flat upper lip.) Leave the form on the bat until the outer ring no longer shines with wetness. At this point, cover the outer ring with plastic, leaving the foot uncovered.

10. When the foot ring is leather hard, turn the form over (or right side up) onto a trimming bat. Center the form on the bat. Then, using a loop trimming tool and metal rib, trim and correct the interior shape of the bowl (Photo 13).

13

11. To smooth the bowl interior, use a flexible metal rib (Photo 14).

14

12. Using a knife, carve through and/or into the outer wall as desired (Photo 15). Then dry the form slowly, flipping it over and rotating it every hour or so until it's ready to paint with slips or to bisque fire.

15

13. Paint the bowl with slips and engobes if you wish.

14. Fire the piece on kiln shelves dusted with sand or fine grog, or on a perfectly flat shrink slab.

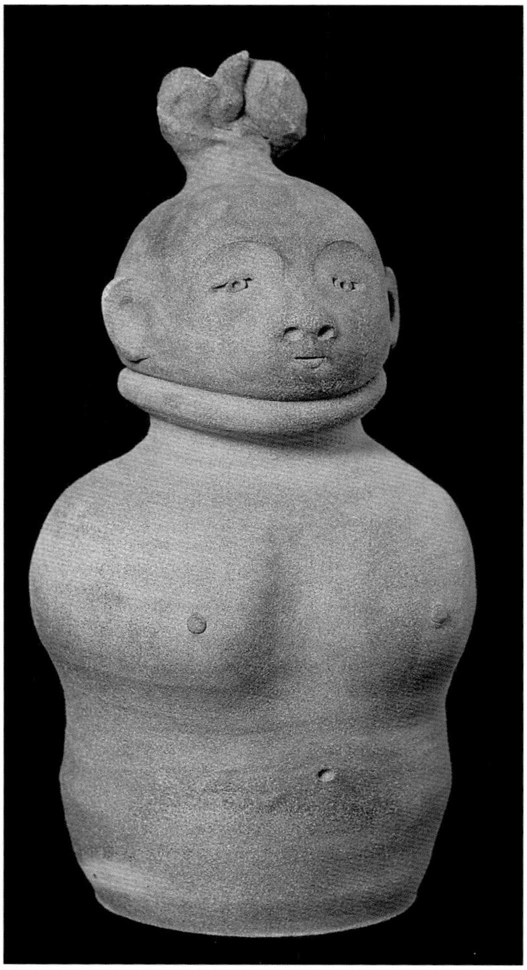

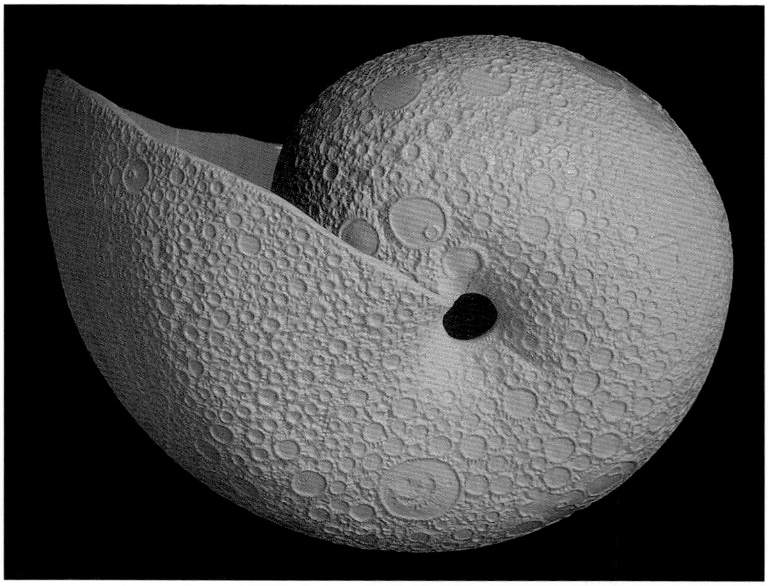

Top left: **Ben Owen,** ***Traditional Candlesticks,*** late 1950s
Height: 14" (35.5 cm). Stoneware; frogskin glaze. Ben Owen was employed as Master Potter at Jugtown Pottery from 1926-1959. Photo courtesy of Sid Oakley and the Museum of American Pottery

Bottom left: **James and Wendy McNally,** ***Pubescent Female,*** 1996
16" x 8" x 7" (40.5 x 20.5 x 18 cm). Stoneware; torso thrown with collared opening, body features added or impressed, thrown head added on; facial features added, molded, and impressed; oxidation fired to cone 8. Photo by Peter Courchesne

Bottom right: **Laurie Childers,** ***Moon Shell,*** 1990
12½" x 12" x 10½" (32 x 30.5 x 26.5 cm). Porcelain; thrown with very thin walls surrounding small hole at top, sliced vertically when stiff, inverted into bisqued chuck, stretched and shaped with Sri Lankan stone anvil and paddle, excess clay removed and some added to interior bottom of spiral wall; carved when dry; glazed interior, thinly sponge-glazed exterior; fired in electric kiln to cone 4. Photo by artist

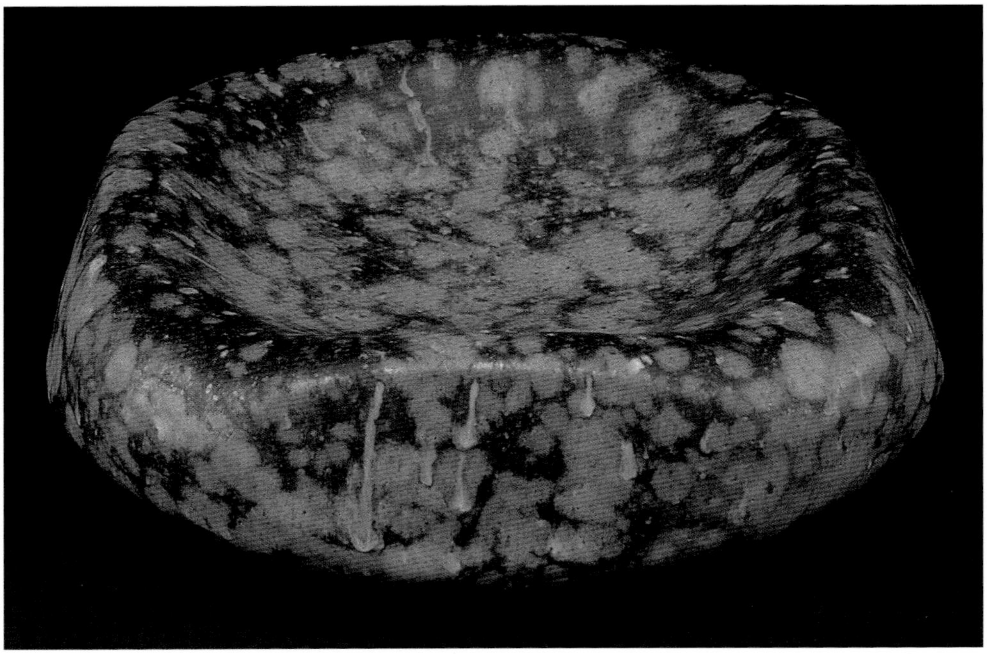

Top: **Sadashi Inuzuka, from "*Nature of Things,*" (600-piece installation),** 1995
Sizes vary. Red earthenware; most pieces thrown, then cut and rolled; sprayed terra sigillata; fired in gas kiln to cone 04.
Photo by Ken Mayer

Top right: **Marla Bollak, *Double Walled Bowl with Tear,*** 1997
4" x 8" x 8" (10 x 20.5 x 20.5 cm). Stoneware; double walls thrown in one piece, inverted "V" imprinted in soft clay to form "belly," rim torn when leather hard and extended to inner and outer wall along belly line; glaze and slip; soda fired, very mild reduction, to cone 10.
Photo by David Caras

Bottom right: **Hiroshi Nakayama, *Vessel,*** 1997
3" x 10" x 10" (7.5 x 25.5 x 25.5 cm). High-fire stoneware; thrown to balloon shape, then altered; multiple glaze layers; reduction fired in gas kiln to cone 10

Top left: **Lisa Mandelkern,** ***Mesilla (teapot),*** 1995
8" x 6½" x 4½" (20.5 x 16 x 11.5 cm). White earthenware; thrown, with hand-built additions; majolica and other glazes; fired in electric kiln to cone 06. Photo by artist

Top right: **Shigeru Miyamoto,** ***Transflux,*** 1996
38½" x 8½" x 8½" (98 x 21.5 x 21.5 cm). Stoneware; press-molded head, base and upper section thrown and joined with extruded tube; wax resist, glaze, stain, and slips; fired in gas kiln, light reduction, to cone 9, followed by short oxidation; head raku fired. Photo by Shuzo Uemoto

Left: **Donna Anderegg,** ***Bottle,*** 1997
7" x 5" x 5" (18 x 12.5 x 12.5 cm). Porcelain; body thrown, trimmed while soft, rolled and slapped to alter shape; lid hand-built; slips applied to bone-dry ware; salt fired to cone 9-10. Photo by artist

CHAPTER FIVE

SURFACE TREATMENTS

Bennett Bean, *Drunken Lily,* 1996
15" x 9½" x 15" (38 x 24 x 38 cm). Earthenware; thrown and altered; bisque fired; tape resist, glazed; pit fired; painted, gold-leaf interior

Surface Treatments

Although you may view throwing as the most exciting part of the pottery-making process, it's important to remember that throwing is indeed only one part. Confronting that soft, impressionable, spinning hunk of moist clay on the wheel; knowing that it's full of exotic possibilities; sliding your hands around it; pushing, pulling, and ultimately blending in glorious harmony with it to create a brand new wet, shimmering piece is—well—like no other experience. Many potters find their pots most beautiful at this stage, but after the pieces have dried and lost their once wet luster, it becomes obvious that the process is not yet complete.

When your beautiful thrown piece is bone dry, it will be a bit dull in appearance, as if it had lost some of its life force. I like to think that a pot at this stage is just dormant—that it's waiting to be brought back to life and further enhanced through a surface treatment and final firing.

These final steps are sometimes daunting to the student. A faulty glaze application or bad firing can ruin your thrown piece. Jumping right in and testing available glazes and other surface treatments as you learn to throw will help your surface treatments develop as part of the process. Once you begin to develop a working familiarity with surface-treatment materials, this part of claywork will become quite exciting, and you'll begin to visualize the final surface treatment as—or even before—you throw a piece.

In fired ceramic ware, no applied material is totally and only "about" the surface. Even if we could, most potters would shudder to focus only on the surface of a piece. Potters start with the form and deal with the surface treatment last. Viewers, however, usually respond to the surface treatment when they first see a pot. A shiny, colorful glaze gets noticed right away. Then, if we're lucky, the other elements of the piece are revealed as equally important qualities. (This fact isn't necessarily negative—just interesting to me.)

The clay will affect whatever is melted onto it. A transparent blue glaze applied to a white porcelain clay body, for example, will have a brilliant quality that can't be attained by applying the same glaze to a dark brown stoneware. These effects are more than a matter of background color. Even opaque matt glazes are influenced by the type of clay to which they're applied. Some glazes will appear richer on one type of clay than on another because there's an area of interface where the clay and glaze mix together. The higher the firing temperature and the more melting that takes place, the more dramatic this mixing will be.

Although fired ceramic surfaces may be painted, and many artists do this, this chapter covers only surface treatments that are fired with the clay. I use the term "surface treatment" because glazes aren't the only option. Engobes, terra sigillata, metallic colorant mixtures, underglazes, the clay itself, and the various firing techniques are all alternatives that can bring forth rich results.

If you're taking a class or working in an art center, you'll probably use premixed surface-treatment materials rather than mixing your own. The application method you use is just as significant to the outcome of your work as any other factor in the pottery-making process. Different students are likely get different results, even when they use the same glaze out of the same bucket and even if their pieces are fired in the same kiln load.

Testing Glazes

Test glazes and other surface treatments before using them on your best pieces. Record in a notebook what you do each time and any ideas you might have for your next attempts. To make test tiles, throw a wide, low cylinder (12 inches or 30.5 cm wide and 4 inches or 10 cm tall is ideal), using the same clay body that you plan to use for your pots. Make sure that the cylinder wall leans slightly inward so that after you've sliced it, each piece will stand on its own when it's fired. When the cylinder is leather hard, slice it up into 12 pieces, just as you would slice a pie. (Each slice will be L-shaped because it will have a bottom as well as a wall.) Make a hole in the bottom so that you can hang up and save each tile that you glaze and fire successfully. An alternative to making these test tiles is to throw a bunch of small cylinders for practice and use them instead.

Surface-Treatment Formulas

Many formulas are available for all kinds of surface treatments (see pages 154-156 for examples). If you plan to mix your own surface-treatment materials, start with a formula for a treatment that will "fit" your type of clay and its firing range. Formulas always include this information, as well as a list of dry ingredients by percentage of weight. The base mixture for a typical formula will add up to 100; if a colorant is called for, it's usually noted at the end of the formula as a percentage addition.

If your glaze doesn't fit your clay, it may shrink at a rate dramatically different from the clay and will "shiver" or "craze." Shivering occurs when the glaze shrinks less than the clay and falls off during the cooling phase of firing. Crazing occurs when the glaze shrinks more than the clay, and small cracks appear through the glaze during cooling.

Another testing concern is glaze absorbency. Some glazes will absorb liquids after firing, even though they appear to have melted. These wouldn't be appropriate on functional ware.

If you're new to mixing your own surface-treatment materials, choose simple recipes that have no more than four or five ingredients in the base mixture, and keep your variety of glazes and other treatments down to a manageable number so that storing ingredients and mixed glazes doesn't pose problems. Store all wet mixtures and dry ingredients in covered containers.

Mixing Surface-Treatment Materials

Start by making sure you have the items listed under "Tools for Glazing" on pages 10-11. Then determine how much you want to mix. One or two hundred grams of dry ingredients will be enough for a colorant mixture for brushing or sponging onto your piece or for a glaze test. For an engobe or a small batch of glaze, 1,000 grams yields an adequate amount and fits into a 1-gallon (3.8 l) bucket. To fill a 5-gallon (19 l) bucket with glaze, 10,000 grams will be about right. I mix my glazes in 10- and 20-pound (4.5 and 9 kg) batches, because it's more convenient for me. For weighing, a triple-beam balance scale is best for gram measurements, and an accurate postal scale works well for pounds.

Now, with the formula next to your scale and your respirator on, place one of the plastic containers on the scale and adjust the scale to zero. Scoop the first ingredient into the container, check it off the formula, and transfer it to a mixing bucket. Repeat to measure all the dry ingredients. Then dry-mix the ingredients with the spatula or ladle. I do this in front of my spray booth so that it will exhaust the dust out of the studio.

Now add water and stir the mixture again. For large batches, an electric drill with a mixer attachment is helpful. Small amounts can be mixed with electric blenders or with a ladle, rubber spatula, or spoon.

Until you become familiar with the surface-treatment concoction you're mixing, deciding exactly how much water to add is tricky. Due to the nature of their different ingredients, two different formulas of the same weight often require different amounts of water. Glazes are usually mixed to the consistency of thick cream, engobes to a slightly thicker consistency, and oxide solutions for brushwork or spraying to a slightly thinner one. The exact consistency required by your work will be an individual matter. Experience with testing and using these surface treatments will help.

It's best to add too little water to the dry ingredients rather than too much. After sieving the mixed glaze (the next step), you can always add more water to get the right consistency. A solution that's too thin won't have the desired effect when it's applied and fired on the ware. If you're working with a small volume of glaze and you've added too much water, you can evaporate some of the water by heating the mixture. If you've added too much water to a large volume, let the mixture settle for a day or two and ladle the excess water off the top. Most ceramic materials aren't water-soluble; they float in suspension and will eventually settle to the bottom of the container. (Be sure to stir any mixture thoroughly before applying it.)

After mixing in the water, set your 60-mesh sieve over another bucket and pour the mixture into the sieve, helping it through with a kitchen brush. Stir in more water if necessary.

Application Methods

First, make sure that your ware is at the right stage of dryness for the treatment you plan to use. Some treatments are formulated for use only on damp or leather-hard ware, some for use on bone-dry ware, and some for use on bisqued ware.

Bring a 1-gallon (3.8 l) bucket of water and a small sponge (natural elephant ear sponges are best) to your glazing area for wiping drips and rinsing your hands. Also use a household sponge to wipe off the surface you'll be working on; do this when you're finished, too. Don't use your glaze-application sponge to wipe the table; it will wear it out. Remember not to dump surface-treatment materials down the sink; they'll clog the drains just as clay will. Wash your hands with soap and water after handling any glaze materials.

If you're glazing bisqued ware, check it over and remove any unwanted bumps or sharp spots by scraping the clay with a metal rib. Wipe the piece with a damp sponge to remove any dust.

Glaze materials must be wiped thoroughly off the bottom of your pieces, or they'll stick to the kiln shelf during firing. Using a liquid wax resist, available from ceramic suppliers, is very helpful. Apply the resist with a small sponge or bristle brush and let the resist dry completely, or it won't be effective. (An hour or two is usually sufficient.) Glaze and other materials that land on top of the resist are easily removed with a damp sponge. Wash the brush with warm water and soap before the resist dries. If you wait too long, and the resist dries in your brush, rubbing alcohol will usually get it out.

Dipping

If you have enough glaze, the simplest way to apply it is to hold your piece with glaze tongs and submerge it in the glaze for a few seconds. If you don't have tongs, some pieces can by hand-dipped. Pieces such as bowls, for example, can be dipped one-half at a time. Glaze dries so quickly that by the time you've dipped one half and put the piece down, you can usually hold the already-dipped portion and dip the other half. For overlapped glaze patterns, just overlap the glaze, doubling its thickness in some areas.

One cautionary note: If a glaze coating is too thick, it may run off the pot during firing, or "crawl," leaving bare spots on your piece. If the glaze you've applied cracks apart as it dries, you'll know it's too thick. Wash it off, let the piece dry, thin your glaze, and start over.

Dipping works best for glazing bisque-fired ware, but can also be used to apply engobes. I have a large aluminum bowl that I use for dipping forms that are too large to dip into my 5-gallon (19 l) glaze buckets.

When the interior of a piece will be glazed differently from the outside, apply the interior glaze first (see the next section).

Pouring

Pouring is a handy application technique for the interiors of pieces. When I glaze the interiors of my pots with a transparent colored glaze, for example, I mix the glaze thin and after pouring some into the pot, I roll the glaze around in the pot twice. This minimizes the effect of overlapping, while also keeping the glaze from being applied too thickly. Then I pour the glaze out and wipe away any drips with a sponge.

Pouring is also effective for glazing exteriors. Hold the piece upside down over the bucket or set it on a couple of sticks that span the container. Using a plastic freezer container, pitcher, or ladle, pour the glaze over the outside of the piece, moving the container around the piece to distribute the glaze evenly and covering the piece completely once or twice. When the glaze stops dripping, turn the piece upright. The rim can be wiped and treated in a different way or quickly dipped in the same glaze.

Pouring is a technique that's usually used with glazes on bisque-fired ware, but may also be used to apply engobes to either bisqued ware or greenware.

Brushing

This application technique may be used with any of the surface treatments and on greenware or bisqued ware. When you're coating a piece with glaze by brushing on the glaze, you can minimize the effects of overlapping by applying several layers. Your brush marks won't show as much.

With underglaze painting or any other brush design in which the brushwork stands out, the flow of the marks you make is critical. Brush marks will always show to some degree, so they should be deliberately made. I often practice on paper or the table top before I make brush marks on a pot.

Adding a ceramic gum to any mixture will help it brush on more fluidly. This is especially helpful on bisqued ware, which is very absorbent. Gums usually come in powdered form and are either included in the solution when you dry-mix it or blended with hot water and added to the solution later.

In order to accentuate a texture, oxide solutions and glazes may be brushed into the recessed areas on bisqued ware and then wiped off the higher surfaces with a damp sponge.

Trailing

Plastic squeeze bottles filled with thick engobe or glaze can be used to draw, squiggle, or fling the surface-treatment material onto your piece. Hair-dye bottles, available from beautician-supply stores, work well. The trailing technique can produce a wide variety of marks, from controlled to very loose, depending on how you move and how you apply the material. What I like about trailing (besides the beautiful marks) is that it can be done in a way that gives me only part of the control—and chance the rest.

Trailing can be done on damp, dry, or bisqued ware, as long as the material you're applying is formulated for the state of the clay.

Spraying

Any of the surface treatments can be sprayed. Spraying requires a compressor. The ones with tanks attached work best and are sure to deliver enough even pressure to your airbrush or spray gun. An airbrush is best for thin solutions such as oxide sprays and for applying solutions to small areas such as rims and handles. Larger sprayers with canisters are better for applying thicker solutions such as engobes and glazes and for covering large areas.

Use a banding wheel to keep the piece rotating as you spray or move the sprayer around in order to prevent overspraying an area. The material should dry quickly, without running. Getting a feel for how thick a sprayed application should be will take some testing. A sprayed glaze coating will appear thicker than a dipped coating because a sprayed coating is pebbly in texture. Sprayed oxides, on the other hand, should be applied comparatively thinly.

Always wear a respirator when you spray and use a spray booth with an exhaust fan. Sprayed surface treatments are especially fragile, so handle your pieces very carefully. Adding a ceramic gum to your mixture will help to toughen the surface somewhat.

Sponging

Any surface treatment can be sponged on for a textured effect. (A sea sponge with irregular cells makes the most interesting texture.) Glazes and oxide mixtures may also be applied by other means and then partly removed with a damp sponge. This is especially effective with oxide mixtures sprayed onto bisqued ware.

Layering and Overlapping

Any surface treatment that melts will mix to some degree with another that it overlaps. Fluid glossy glazes will melt and mix the most; dry engobes will melt and mix the least. A glaze that overlaps another glaze won't just cover it. Some mixing will occur when they melt. Although engobes will mix when they've been poured or brushed over one another in their wet state, if the bottom layer is allowed to dry to leather hard before the top layer is applied, the top will cover the bottom pretty thoroughly. Overlapped oxide sprays and underglazes will mix and sometimes become muddy looking when they're overlapped.

Resists

Masking tape, wax resist, and liquid latex can all be used for resist effects on bisqued ware. Wax resist can also yield good results when it's brushed on after applying a glaze and allowed to dry before dipping the piece in a contrasting glaze. Liquid latex is handy for masking an area before applying a surface treatment; it's peeled off afterwards to leave the area exposed for another treatment. Paper may also be used for resist patterns (see pages 93-94).

Surface Treatments

In this section, you'll find descriptions of a variety of surface treatments and instructions for their use. Some are best applied to bisque-fired clay, which is in an ideal state for glaze application. Because the chemical water has been driven out of the clay molecules by the heat of firing, the hardened clay will no longer melt when it's submerged in water, but it will absorb a certain amount of water when it's dipped into a glaze. Water-based surface-treatment materials therefore dry quickly on its surface, and you can wash off any mistakes.

Glazes may be applied to leather-hard clay or to bone-dry greenware, eliminating the need for a bisque firing. Good results are possible but the materials applied need to be tested on the clay first to make sure they fit and produce the desired effect during firing. Your application must be right the first time, as it's difficult to wash glaze off raw (unfired) clay without destroying the piece.

Clay as A Surface Treatment

One possibility is to let the clay itself be a surface treatment. Some clays—rich red or tan clays, for example—are quite pleasing when left exposed and can be especially appealing in sculptural, highly textured, or carved pieces. The type and temperature of the firing will affect the color of the clay (see pages 147-149).

Some potters make marbled clay by alternating layers of different colored clay as they prepare the clay for throwing. The layers can be sliced and rejoined in a variety of ways to yield different color patterns. Carving into the leather-hard clay can accentuate this effect. If you combine colored clays, be sure to test a small piece through the drying and firing cycles to make sure the clays shrink at the same rate and don't crack apart. Pieces made in this manner are sometimes called "agate ware" and can be attractive left unglazed or coated with a transparent glaze.

Terra Sigillata

Terra sigillata is made up of very fine clay particles mixed with water and what's known as a deflocculant, and may be used with or without colorants. (See Appendix E on page 156 for a terra sigillata formula and mixing instructions.) It's brushed or sprayed onto bone-dry ware and is usually burnished. It's then fired in a low-temperature firing (cone 06 to cone 3) because it tends to lose its burnished sheen at higher temperatures. Terra sigillata was originally used to seal clay surfaces before glazes were discovered. Glazes aren't applied over it because they would cover its pleasant eggshell-like texture.

Engobes

The word "slip" is often used interchangeably with the word engobe. I prefer to use "engobe" because it pertains only to the liquid clay mixture that is applied to a pot after it is made in order to serve as a surface design element. The word "slip" is used to describe several different types of liquid clay, including that which is poured into molds for casting.

An engobe may be the color of the clay with which it's made or may include one of a wide variety of added colorants. (See Appendix B on page 155 for some engobe formulas.)

Depending on how they're formulated, engobes are applied to damp clay, to bone-dry clay, or to bisqued ware. I find that brushing an engobe onto damp or leather-hard clay is far more pleasant than applying it to dry or bisqued ware and also affords design possibilities unique to the damp phase of clay: combing designs through the engobe, trailing and "feathering" the engobe from a squeeze bottle, and applying engobes over paper resist.

The relatively high clay content of engobes causes them to shrink quite a bit as they dry. Because they do shrink, they must be matched to the ware. An engobe formulated for application to wet or damp ware, for example, must shrink along with the clay as it dries, or it will crack off. When engobes are applied thickly, any shrinkage problems will be amplified. Engobes for dry or bisqued ware are formulated for minimal shrinkage in order to fit. An engobe and pot must also shrink at a similar rate during the final firing, or the engobe may flake off. One way to avoid this problem when you're throwing with a whiteware or porcelain clay is to mix an engobe with the same clay, adding colorants to it. Applying some of the engobe to a test piece and firing it first can prevent sad results on your best pieces.

Engobes may be applied by brushing, trailing, pouring, or spraying, and may be used with or without a glaze coating over them.

Metallic Colorants

Metallic colorants, which are added in small amounts to glazes and engobes, include iron, cobalt, copper, chrome, manganese, nickel, and a few others, and are available as oxides, carbonates, and sulfates. Oxides and carbonates are preferable, as sulfates are water soluble, which makes them hazardous and difficult to use. Avoid getting metallic colorants on your hands or breathing their dust, as they're potentially poisonous. Always wear a respirator and use a scoop or a spoon to remove dry colorants from their containers.

Metallic colorants may also be mixed in concentrated solutions and sprayed, brushed, or sponged on. These may be fired without a glaze coating over them for a "dry" look or treated as underglaze colors by covering them with a transparent glaze. They're very difficult to handle before firing, however, as they smudge easily. Adding a ceramic gum helps prevent this. (For formulas, see Appendix D on page 156.)

Commercial Stains and Underglazes

Stains consist of metallic colorants mixed with other ingredients that help regulate the color, quality of melt, and ease of application. They come in powdered form and are available from ceramic suppliers. In many ways, they're similar in quality to commercially prepared glazes, but they're usually more opaque than glazes and tend to coat the clay with colors that are flatter in appearance than the raw oxide and carbonate mixtures. Stains may be added to glazes or engobes and used in any way that metallic colorants are used.

Commercial underglazes are available from ceramic suppliers in a wide variety of colors that are premixed with water and packaged in small bottles. These are applied as the name implies (under a glaze), as well as on top of a glaze or without a glaze for a dry look. Underglaze color charts are available, but do test underglazes on your clay and in your firing before using them on your best pieces.

Glazes

Volumes have been written on the subject of glazes, and because the focus of this book is on throwing, I won't attempt to explain glaze formulation or technology in any great depth here. Instead, I offer the following information in order to help introduce you to the basic concepts.

Clay and glazes are essentially the same. They're both made of alumina and silica, with other modifying ingredients that affect the melting temperature, texture, strength, color, and other qualities. The balance among these three components determines the quality of the material. Alumina provides body, opacity, and stiffness. Silica forms glass. Clay is high in alumina, and glazes are high in silica.

Another important fact about glazes is that when any two of their ingredients are ground and mixed together, they'll melt at a lower temperature than the highest melting point of the individual ingredients.

On one level, glaze composition is quite simple. On another, a person could spend several lifetimes calculating and testing the infinite number of ingredient combinations that are possible. Folk potters traditionally glazed with ingredients accessible to them locally: wood ash, clay, ground quartz or limestone, and glass fragments, without being very scientific in their approach. They tested proportions until the glaze melted properly on the local clay. On a few fortunate occasions, crushed local stone or clay satisfied the criteria for a good glaze and melted well without added ingredients.

Today, many refined glaze materials are readily available, and it's up to the individual potter to decide how deeply he or she wishes to become involved in experimenting with glaze composition. The surface treatments that seem to be most appropriate for the potter's own expressions will be the determining factor.

Lusters and Overglaze Enamels

These materials, which are available from ceramic-supply stores, are applied over fired glazes and fired once again to a lower temperature (cone 018 to cone 022) than the glaze over which they're applied.

Firing Methods

Firing is the ultimate surface treatment. No matter how a piece is thrown or treated with engobes, glazes, or colorants, the firing will determine how these elements turn out. In fact, firing influences every aspect of a ceramic piece. We always hope, of course, that the clay and surface-treatment materials will fuse together in glorious harmony in the fire. This goal is sometimes elusive, but you'll almost certainly reach it often enough to lead you on to the next kiln load.

One firing is distinguished from another by several factors:

- Whether a kiln is used, and if so, what kind. Unlike mid-range and high-temperature firings, which can only take place in a kiln because only a kiln will retain sufficient heat, some low-temperature firings, such as pit-firing, don't require a kiln.
- The fuel used to fire the kiln
- The maximum temperatures reached inside the kiln. Different clays and glazes require different maximum firing temperatures in order to reach maturity.
- How quickly the kiln reaches the desired maximum temperature and how quickly or slowly the ware is allowed to cool. A long slow firing and cooling cycle will result in greater vitrification of the clay than a quick firing to the same temperature.
- Whether or not oxygen levels in the kiln are reduced (see the next section)
- Whether or not the clay is fired to maturity, its point of vitrification, and the degree to which the clay vitrifies

Each of these factors influences the final appearance of the piece.

Oxidation and Reduction Firing

Two firing variations that greatly affect the color and quality of the ware are oxidation and reduction firing. Two identical pieces fired to the same temperature, for the same length of time—one in an oxidation atmosphere and one in a reduction atmosphere—can look dramatically different.

An oxidation firing, as its name implies, is one in which oxygen is present in the kiln. This is probably the easiest type of firing, especially when the potter is using an electric kiln. Although oxidation-fired surface-treatment colors tend to be brilliant and sometimes even harsh, unique and wonderful results are possible with this firing method.

Reduction firing requires a kiln that runs on a combustible fuel such as gas, wood, or oil. (Gas and other combustible fuels may also be used for oxidation firing.) By reducing the amount of oxygen available to these fuels as they burn, oxygen is actually borrowed from the heated clay and glaze ingredients. The oxygen must be reduced at certain stages of the firing; this is done either by closing the damper at the base of the stack or by lessening the air intake at the burner or fire box. This in turn causes chemical and color changes in the ware and surface-treatment materials. Iron in the clay, for example, turns a warm tan or grey color; in a celadon glaze, iron turns light green or blue. Only in a reduction firing will the copper in a glaze yield brilliant, copper red.

Some colors may burn out or become muted in a reduction firing, but this firing method offers a great deal of variety from piece to piece. In addition, because the potter must take an active role in monitoring a reduction firing, the process offers an added excitement and involvement that's not generally present during electric-kiln firings. The warm magic that it makes possible shows through in the finished ware.

Raku Firing

Raku firing is quite popular because it offers quick results and some dazzling glaze effects. The ware is first bisque fired and glazed with a low-temperature glaze (cone 012 to cone 04). Then it's placed in a small kiln and heated quickly. When the glaze has melted, the ware is removed from the kiln and placed in a combustible material such as newspaper or straw, and covered. Raku setups vary. Some potters use metal garbage cans with lids. (Some actual glaze reduction is possible at this stage if the glaze is still molten enough when the piece is placed in the can.)

On unglazed areas of a piece, the carbon in the smoke produced by raku firing darkens the clay. Pieces with clear glazes can produce an elegant black crackle effect. The glaze appears white due to the light-colored clay behind it. The carbon in the smoke penetrates the cracks in the glaze to blacken the clay, creating a web of dark lines. The cracks form as the glaze cools and shrinks a little more than the clay. Other more subtle effects can be created by using engobes or oxides containing small amounts of copper, iron, or rutile instead of glaze, and using less combustible material. Many other variations on the raku technique are used for specialized results. Because the finished ware is porous and smoky, it's rarely used as functional or utilitarian ware.

The raku firing method just described is the "Americanized" version of the original Japanese method, and its invention is credited to Paul Soldner. Japanese raku pieces are fired at higher temperatures, removed from the kiln while still glowing hot, and allowed to cool rapidly. Japanese raku-fired pieces aren't smoked or reduced, however, and the technique is often used to create tea bowls and other utilitarian ware.

Ware stacked and ready to fire after the surface treatments have been completed. The pieces sit on shelves that are separated by posts. The floor and door of this car kiln roll in and out on tracks.
Photo by (and kiln of) Don Davis

Salt Glazing and Wood Firing

Salt glazing (a process that takes place during firing) and wood firing both require fewer prefiring surface treatments than any other firing method, but they do require more attention from the potter, who must orchestrate the firing itself.

The interiors of salt-fired and wood-fired ware are usually glazed to insure their usability, while engobes, metallic colorants, and glazes may or may not be used to enhance their exterior surfaces.

Wood firing and salt glazing are experiencing a tremendous resurgence of popularity among studio potters today, because both methods offer natural ways to impart a rich and varied surface to the ware through the action of the fire. Work fired by these methods can be quite beautiful, with many subtle variations in texture and tone.

Several types of kilns designed for wood firing exist, from the groundhog kiln design used by the traditional folk potters of the southern United States to the Japanese climbing kilns. In any wood-fired kiln, flames and wood ash flowing through the kiln and contacting the ware create the desired effect. A long wood-firing, lasting for several days, will have a greater effect on the ware than a shorter one.

Before fuel oil and gas were available, all kilns were fired with wood, coal, brush, or dung. For high-temperature firings and maximum clay vitrification, however, early potters found that wood produced the most intense heat and was most efficient in attaining the required temperature. Some of the finest traditional wood-fired work produced is the Iga, Shigaraki, Tamba, and Bizen ware of Japan, in which flame and wood-ash effects have been used to great advantage for hundreds of years. Indeed, these Japanese wares are the main inspiration for most wood firers around the world today.

A view of the fired ware on the bottom shelf of the kiln.
Photo by Don Davis.

Other early potters protected their pieces from the flames and ash of wood-fired kilns by encasing them in saggars (lidded cylinders made of clay). This is how fine celadon glazes, underglaze decoration, and copper reds were produced in antiquity. Inside the saggar, the piece received the benefits of the high heat and atmosphere in the kiln, but the elegant glazes were not muddied by the licking flames and fly ash.

Salt glazing, which originated in Germany in the fifteenth century, is the process of introducing salt (NaCl) into the kiln when the clay in the kiln has reached maturity, usually through small openings above the burner ports. Its classic effect is a smooth but slightly bumpy glaze, with a texture somewhat like that of an orange peel.

This glazing method produces extremely corrosive vapors that would quickly ruin the elements in an electric kiln, so salt glazing is only executed in kilns that make use of a combustible fuel source. The salt vaporizes in the kiln, and the sodium in the vapor combines with the silica in the clay to form a glaze on the surface of the ware. The chlorine becomes a gas, billows out of the kiln, and combines with water vapor in the air. The vapors from a salt kiln disperse quite rapidly, and air pollution is minimal. Concerns about the dangerous vapors, however, have led many potters to substitute sodium bicarbonate for part or all of the salt, with reasonably good results.

A combination of wood firing and salt glazing can produce some exquisite results. The combined effect of the flames, fly ash and salt can provide a very seductive surface treatment.

Left: **Unknown,** ***Japanese Oribe Sake Set,*** 19th century
Bottle height: 5" (12.5 cm). Stoneware; thrown freely and dented; iron wash brushwork often inspired by textile designs, clear and Oribe green glaze; protected in a saggar from ash during oxidation wood firing. The spontaneous asymmetrical harmony achieved in Oribe ware has inspired many contemporary potters. Collection of Don Davis, photo by Evan Bracken

Bottom left: **Patricia L. Hankins,** ***Keep,*** 1995
3" x 2" x 2" (7.5 x 5 x 5 cm). Stoneware; thrown as closed form, beaten with wooden spoon when leather hard, feet and lid cut out, knob made from beads threaded on copper wire; surface marks made with red peppers, copper wire, rabbit food, and marigolds; terra sigillata; bisque fired to cone 022; saggar fired in gas kiln to cone 07. Photo by Bart's Art

Bottom right: **Don Davis,** ***Tripod Jar,*** 1997
Height: 9" (23 cm). Porcelain; thrown with hand-built additions; bisque fired to cone 06; tape resist pattern and sprayed metallic colorant solutions; glaze fired to cone 7, light reduction. Photo by Tim Barnwell

Right: **Paul Soldner,** ***Untitled***
27" x 28" x 16" (69 x 71 x 41 cm). Thrown and handbuilt; low-temperature salt fired

Bottom left: **Michael Simon,** ***Persian Jar,*** 1995
5" x 5" x 4" (12.5 x 12.5 x 10 cm). Stoneware; thrown and reshaped; once-fired to cone 10 in a salted reduction kiln. Collection of Highwater Clays; photo by Evan Bracken

Bottom right: **Ginny Marsh,** ***Vase,*** 1995
6½" x 4½" x 4½" (16.5 x 11.5 x 11.5 cm). Porcelain; thrown, faceted with fettling knife when stiff, and trimmed; copper and rutile glaze; reduction fired in gas kiln to cone 9. Photo by artist

Top left: **Colleen Zufelt, *Mardi Gras,*** 1996
24" x 16" x 16" (61 x 40.5 x 40.5 cm). Low-fire white clay; body thrown, joined to slab top; lid hand-built; airbrushed velvets and underglazes over stencils, tape resist, graphic press-applied stickers, penciled underglaze accents; once fired in electric kiln to cone 04; cast feet fired and epoxied in place; drawing surface sealed with fixative.
Photo by Carson Zullinger

Top right: **Shari Sikora, *Mustard T-Pot,*** 1997
9½" x 5½" x 5½" (24 x 14 x 14 cm). Porcelain; thrown; surfaces textured with pencil and needle tool when leather hard; tape resist, copper glazes and clear textured areas; raku fired. Photo by John Carlano

Bottom left: **Laura Nuchols, *Origami Cranes,*** 1995
18" x 18" x 2" (45.5 x 45.5 x 5 cm). Porcelain; thrown; foot added with coil, then thrown; slip applied to greenware, wax resist design carved through slip; bisque fired; glaze fired in electric kiln to cone 10. Photo by David Andersen

Top: **Lori Mills, *Tulip Barge—Double Decker,*** 1997
17½" x 21" x 7" (44.5 x 53.5 x 18 cm). Terra-cotta; thrown bottomless cylinder stretched into oval, added leaves, slab bottom, with hand-built additions; slips brushed, trailed, and carved through; bisque fired; glazed; fired in electric kiln to cone 05-04

Right: **Cynthia L. Young, *"Ode to Coffee"* Wall Piece,** 1997
20" x 20" x 6" (51 x 51 x 15 cm). Red earthenware; thrown and tossed at an angle before leather hard; dipped and brushed slips and glazes; oxidation fired to cone 05. Photo by Peter Shefler

Appendix A: Glaze Formulas

Warning! Silver nitrate and barium carbonate, which are included in a few of these formulas, are very toxic. Wear a respirator and rubber gloves with neoprene (the heavy blue gloves) when handling, mixing, and applying the glazes. Silver nitrate also leaves nasty brown stains wherever it lands, so be careful.

Don's Clear (from the author)
Cone 5-7; oxidation or reduction

EPK (Florida kaolin)	7.5
F-4 feldspar	25.0
Silica	27.5
Dolomite	5.0
Whiting	5.0
Gerstley borate	10.0
Frit 3124	20.0
	100%

For blue, add 1% cobalt carbonate. (I use this on interiors and call it "Blue Liner.")

Randy's Green Glaze Revised (from the author)
Cone 7-10

F-4 feldspar	19.0
K-200 feldspar	23.0
Ball clay	17.0
Whiting	9.5
Dolomite	7.0
Barium carbonate	13.5
Silica	17.0
	100%

Add 6% copper carbonate and 12% Zircopax.

Clear Crackle (from the author)
Cone 5-7; oxidation or reduction

Nepheline syenite	38.0
K-200 feldspar	8.0
EPK (Florida kaolin)	7.0
325-mesh silica	23.0
Gerstley borate	15.0
Whiting	9.0
	100%

For copper red, add .5% copper carbonate and 1.5% tin oxide, and reduction fire.

MC Matt Revised (from the author)
Cone 5-7; oxidation or reduction

Nepheline syenite	60.0
Lithium carbonate	1.0
Strontium carbonate	20.0
Ball clay	10.0
Silica	9.0
	100%

For blue-green, add 5% copper carbonate.

Before adding water, add 1% bentonite and 1% V-Gum Cer, and dry-mix the ingredients thoroughly.

Separating Glaze (from the author)
Cone 5-7; oxidation or reduction

Nepheline syenite	70.0
Magnesium carbonate	30.0
	100%

Add 5% bentonite.

Remember: Always test surface treatments before using them on your finished pieces. See pages 142-143 for instructions.

Shino, Carbon Trap (from the author)
Cone 7-10; reduction

Nepheline syenite	68.5
OM4 ball clay	18.0
EPK (Florida kaolin)	4.5
Soda ash	4.5
Spodumene	4.5
	100%

Chun Clear (from Leah Leitson)
Cone 5-6; oxidation

Soda spar (F-4)	38.0
Whiting	14.0
Zinc oxide	12.0
Ball clay	6.0
Flint	30.0
	100%

For blue celadon, add .5% copper.

For yellow, add 4% 6464 mason stain.

Glaze—NSA8; clear glossy (from Norm Schulman)
Cone 3

Ferro frit 3124	70.0
Barium carbonate	2.0
Lithium carbonate	2.0
Flint	16.0
Kaolin	5.0
Whiting	5.0
	100%

For opaque glossy enamel, add 10% Ultrox.

To aid suspension, add 2% Macaloid or VeeGum.

To prevent glaze from dusting, add 1 tablespoon per gallon (or 3.8 l) CMC.

Lithium Blue Satin Raku (from Steve Forbes-deSoule)
Cone 06-05

Silica	54.6
Lithium carbonate	27.8
Kaolin	12.1
Soda ash	3.5
Bentonite	1.0
Bone ash	1.0
	100%

Add 3.7% copper carbonate.

Seth's Luster (raku glaze from Rick Berman)
Matt copper luster, excellent over Lithium Blue Satin Raku
Cone 06-05

Gerstley borate	80.0
Bone ash	20.0
	100%

Add 10% copper carbonate, 5% cobalt carbonate, and 1.3% tin oxide.

Copper Emerald Green Raku (from Steve Forbes-deSoule)
Cone 06-05

Frit 3134	43.0
Gerstley borate	38.0
EPK (Florida kaolin)	12.0
Flint	7.0
	100%

Add 6% copper carbonate.

For teal, add 0.6% cobalt carbonate.

For black, reduce copper carbonate to 4% and add 5% manganese dioxide, 8% red iron, and 3% cobalt carbonate.

For gold luster, add 3% silver nitrate.

Light Turquoise Copper Raku (from Steve Forbes-deSoule)
Turquoise matt in oxidation; copper luster in reduction
Cone 06-05

Gerstley borate	37.5
Lithium carbonate	23.5
Spodumene	20.0
Zircopax	19.0
	100%

Add 2.4% copper carbonate and .5% Epsom salts.

For medium blue, add 1.2% cobalt carbonate.

Steve's Gold Sand Raku (from Steve Forbes-deSoule)
The secret of this glaze is to look beneath the surface.
Cone 06-05

Frit 3110	85.0
Nepheline syenite	10.0
Kaolin	5.0
	100%

Add 25% natural bone ash and 3% silver nitrate. You may use synthetic bone ash (tri-calcium phosphate), but the results will be different.

Appendix B: Engobe Formulas

Don's Engobe Base (from the author)
Cone 5-7; for wet to leather-hard clay

#6 tile clay (Georgia kaolin)	25.0
EPK (Florida kaolin)	25.0
Ball clay	25.0
Frit 3124	15.0
Nepheline syenite	10.0
	100%

For black, add 2% cobalt oxide, 5% red iron oxide, 5% manganese dioxide, and 3% copper carbonate. Alternatively, add 10% black stain.

For reddish-brown, add 3%-7% red iron oxide.

For white, use base + 2% tin oxide or Zircopax.

For other colors, test 3%-10% colorant.

Don's Copper Sulfate Solution (from the author)
For bisqued porcelain; reduction fired

2 pounds (.9 kg) of copper sulfate per gallon (3.8 l) of water

Wearing rubber gloves, stir well and dip or pour over the ware.

Norm's Engobe—EW7B1 (from Norm Schulman)
Cone 04-10; for bone-dry or bisqued clay

Kaolin	10.0
Custer feldspar	20.0
OM4 ball clay	15.0
Flint	15.0
Whiting	25.0
Zircopax	10.0
Calcined kaolin	5.0
	100%

Add colorants as desired.

Raku Slip Resist #1 (from Steve Forbes-deSoule)
This is applied to the bisqued clay and cracks apart as it dries. When the piece is raku fired, the smoke enters through the cracks. After firing, the slip is scraped off to reveal the smoky pattern.

Fire clay	50.0
EPK (Florida kaolin)	30.0
Aluminum hydrate	20.0
	100%

Raku Slip Resist #2 (from Steve Forbes-deSoule)

Ball clay	40.0
EPK (Florida kaolin)	40.0
Aluminum hydrate	20.0
	100%

For a better hold on vertical surfaces, increase the aluminum hydrate to 23%. For easy removal, decrease it.

Appendix C: Clay Formulas

Don's Porcelaneous Clay (from the author)
Cone 5-7

Tennessee ball clay	22.0
#6 tile clay (Georgia kaolin)	10.0
EPK (Florida kaolin)	10.0
Kaopaque (Georgia kaolin)	7.0
Nepheline syenite	33.0
G-200 feldspar	9.0
Silica	9.0
	100%

Add 1% Vee-Gum T.

Stoneware Clay (from the author)
Cone 7-10

Gold art clay	60.0
Ball clay	20.0
Fire clay	10.0
K-200 feldspar	8.0
Red art clay	2.0
	100%

Clay Body (from Norm Schulman)
Cone 2-5

Kentucky OM4 ball clay	10.0
A.P. green fire clay	30.0
Red art clay	15.0
Foundry Hill Cream	20.0
Lizella Ochmulgee	15.0
Grog (fine fired)	10.0
	100%

Raku Clay Body (from Steve Forbes-deSoule)

Hawthorne fire clay	17.91
Kentucky OM4 ball clay	14.93
XX-Saggar	37.31
#6 tile clay (Georgia kaolin)	14.93
Nepheline syenite (270)	4.48
Kyanite (35-mesh)	1.49
Kyanite (48-mesh)	7.46
Bentonite	1.49
	100%

Appendix D: The Author's Metallic Colorants

Cone 5-10

I apply these to bare clay or under a glaze. To help them melt more, increase the frit and decrease the clay.

Green, Blue-Green, and Blue

Frit 3124	80.0
EPK (Florida kaolin)	20.0
	100%

For green, add 2% cobalt carbonate and 3% chrome oxide.

For blue-green, add 3% cobalt carbonate and 2% chrome oxide.

For blue, add 5% cobalt carbonate.

(Adding 5% V-Gum Cer will help with application and reduce smudging.)

Ochre

Frit 3124	50.0
EPK (Florida kaolin)	50.0
	100%

Add 10% rutile.

Rust

Frit 3124	60.0
EPK (Florida kaolin)	40.0
	100%

Add 10% red iron oxide.

Appendix E: Terra Sigillata

Terra Sigillata (based on information from Mark Burleson)

1 pound (454 g) OM4 ball clay
1 quart (946 ml) water
2 grams sodium silicate

Mix the sodium silicate and water first. Then add the clay. Stir thoroughly again. Allow the mixture to settle overnight, until three layers are visible. Discard the top layer (water); decant the middle layer (terra sigillata); and discard the bottom layer of coarse particles.

To the wet terra sigillata base, add 1 teaspoon of cobalt carbonate (for blue), 1½ teaspoons copper carbonate (for green), or 2 teaspoons red iron oxide (for tan). Other clays and colorants can be used for different effects.

Appendix F: Cone-Firing Ranges

For large, regular Orton cones (270°F or 132°C temperature rise per hour)

Cone Number	Degrees Fahrenheit	Degrees Centigrade
019	1265	685
018	1337	725
017	1386	752
016	1443	784
015	1485	807
014	1528	831
013	1578	859
012	1587	864
011	1623	884
010	1641	894
09	1693	928
08	1751	955
07	1803	984
06	1830	999
05	1915	1046
04	1940	1060
03	2014	1101
02	2048	1120
01	2079	1137
1	2109	1154
2	2124	1162
3	2134	1168
4	2167	1186
5	2185	1196
6	2232	1222
7	2264	1240
8	2305	1263
9	2336	1280
10	2381	1305
11	2399	1315
12	2419	1326

Appendix G: Safety

For accurate information on precautions to take in any ceramic studio, you'll find the following two books, both written by Monona Rossol, very useful:

The Artist's Complete Health and Safety Guide, 2d. Ed. (New York, Allworth Press, 1994) and *Keeping Clay Work Safe and Legal* (Bandon, Oregon: National Council for Education for the Ceramic Arts, 1996).

Metric Conversions

Inches	Cm	Inches	Cm
⅛	0.3	20	50.8
¼	0.6	21	53.3
⅜	1.0	22	55.9
½	1.3	23	58.4
⅝	1.6	24	61.0
¾	1.9	25	63.5
⅞	2.2	26	66.0
1	2.5	27	68.6
1¼	3.2	28	71.1
1½	3.8	29	73.7
1¾	4.4	30	76.2
2	5.1	31	78.7
2½	6.4	32	81.3
3	7.6	33	83.8
3½	8.9	34	86.4
4	10.2	35	88.9
4½	11.4	36	91.4
5	12.7	37	94.0
6	15.2	38	96.5
7	17.8	39	99.1
8	20.3	40	101.6
9	22.9	41	104.1
10	25.4	42	106.7
11	27.9	43	109.2
12	30.5	44	111.8
13	33.0	45	114.3
14	35.6	46	116.8
15	38.1	47	119.4
16	40.6	48	121.9
17	43.2	49	124.5
18	45.7	50	127.0
19	48.3		

Volumes

1 fluid ounce	29.6 ml
1 pint	473 ml
1 quart	946 ml
1 gallon (128 fl. oz.)	3.785 l

Weights

0.035 ounces	1 gram
1 ounce	28.35 grams
1 pound	453.6 grams

Temperatures

To convert fahrenheit to centigrade (Celsius), subtract 32, multiply by 5, and divide by 9.

To convert centigrade (Celsius) to fahrenheit, multiply by 9, divide by 5, and add 32.

Acknowledgments

I view this book as a group effort and would like to thank the many people who helped make it possible.

■ My wife, Marian, and sons, Micah and Will, for their love and encouragement while I was immersed in this project. I thank them, and my parents; my brother, Sparks; and my sister, Judy, for believing in my work.

■ My teachers, who still inspire me: Norm Schulman, Chuck Hindes, Jun Kaneko, Wayne Higby, Phil Ward, and Bill Clover.

■ Rob Pulleyn (owner of Lark Books, Asheville, NC) and Lark's publisher, Carol Taylor, for having provided me with the opportunity to write *Wheel-Thrown Ceramics*. It's been a privilege.

■ The great staff at Lark Books. Special thanks to Chris Rich, my editor, for her friendship and guidance during the writing process. Her unfailing concern, good humor, and professionalism kept me on track and on time. I'm grateful to Lark's art director, Kathy Holmes, for always listening to me while she used her own creative expertise to achieve the best results and for being such a joy to work with.

■ Evan Bracken (Light Reflections, Hendersonville, NC), for his enthusiasm, easy-going nature, and beautiful photos.

■ Clay artists Norm Schulman, Cynthia Bringle, Steve Forbes-deSoule, and Leah Leitson, for having donated their time to demonstrate projects for this book.

■ All the artists who sent in photos of their many wonderful clay pieces. I regret that we couldn't include them all.

■ The many colleagues who so generously shared their time and knowledge with me while I was researching various aspects of this book.

■ Our amazing friends—Leah, Laurel, George, Jackie, Rick, Pat, Julie, Kathy, Olivier, Richard, and Steve—who delivered sustenance in the form of dinners as the intense final stages of completing this book coincided with a family crisis.

■ Thanks also to the Archie Bray Foundation (Helena, MT); Thea Burger (Geneva, IL; agent for Ruth Duckworth); Ruth Butler (editor of *Ceramics Monthly*); Margaret Carney (The International Museum of Ceramic Art at Alfred, The New York State College of Ceramics at Alfred University, Alfred, NY); Laurie Childers (Corvallis, OR); Garth Clark Gallery (New York, NY); Brian Giffin (Giffin Tec, Inc., Boulder, CO); Tom Gray (Seagrove, NC); Highwater Clays (Asheville, NC); Dick Lehman (Goshen, IN); Michael Lemm (Memphis, TN); Ed McEndarfer (Kirksville, MO); Nidec-Shimpo America Corporation, Ceramics Division (Itasca, IL); Sid Oakley (Cedar Creek Gallery, Creedmoor, NC) and the Museum of American Pottery; Ben Owen III (Seagrove, NC); Perimeter Gallery (Chicago, IL); Glenn Rand (Mason, MI); Tom Randall (Rochester, NY); Peter Rose (Knoxville, TN); Marcia Selsor (Billings, MT); Lee Shank (Fernandina Beach, FL); and the Southern Highland Handicraft Guild (Asheville, NC).

Contributing Artists

Don Davis (Davis Studio Pottery), Asheville, NC. Pages 3, 5, 7, 19, 50, 51, 52, 54, 58, 62, 63, 64, 66, 74, 76, 80, 82, 90, 92, 94, 100, 107, 109, 118, 120, 150, and back cover

Anonymous artists. Pages 47 (vase); 56 (soba cup); 78 (Austrian plate); 150 (sake set)

Elaine F. Alt, Marblehead, MA. Page 17

Donna Anderegg, Denver, CO. Page 140

Linda Arbuckle, Micanopy, FL. Page 110

Posey Bacopoulos, New York, NY. Page 111

Carl Baker (Carl Baker, Potter), Crestline, CA. Page 117

Allen Bales (Earth, Fire, Water Studio), Lakewood, CO. Page 20

Bennet Bean, Blairstown, NJ. Pages 17 and 141

Richey Bellinger, Portland, OR. Page 55

Mary Tyson Bertmaring, Rock Hill, SC. Page 130

Charles Fergus Binns (1857-1934). Page 99

Jeanne Bisson (Romulus Craft), Washington, VT. Page 19

Colleen Black-Semelka, Chapel Hill, NC. Page 30

Marla Bollak (Away with Clay), Acton, MA. Page 139

Judy Brater-Rose, Knoxville, TN. Page 18

Lucy Breslin, South Portland, ME. Page 80

Cynthia Bringle, Penland, NC. Pages 50, 66, and 68

Sandra Byers, Rock Springs, WI. Page 97

Winthrop Byers, Rock Springs, WI. Page 78

John F. Byrd, Hendersonville, NC. Page 132

Laurie Childers, Corvallis, OR. Page 138

Robert Bede Clarke, Columbia, MO. Pages 79 and 89

Sam Clarkson, Carrollton, TX. Page 57

Jerry Conrad (Conrad Pottery), Seattle, WA. Page 71

Ginny Conrow (Conrow Porcelain), Seattle, WA. Page 97

Hans Coper, c/o Garth Clark Gallery, New York, NY. Page 67

Burlon Craig, Vale, NC. Page 124

Maggie Creshkoff (The Backlog Pottery), Port Deposit, MD. Page 96

Val M. Cushing (VC Pottery), Alfred, NY. Pages 99 and 124

Malcolm Davis (Malcolm Davis Porcelain), Washington, D.C. Page 56

Dave and Boni Deal, Camas, WA. Page 91

Josh DeWeese, Helena, MT. Page 123

Gerry Dinnen, Carnegie, PA. Page 132

Nathaniel Dixon (1827-1863). Page 30

Ruth Duckworth (c/o Thea Burger Associates, Inc.), Geneva, IL. Page 44

Stephen Fabrico, Bloomington, NY. Page 71

Ken Ferguson, Shawnee, KS. Pages 79 and 123

Marko Fields, Lawrence, KS. Page 110

Steven Forbes-deSoule (Forbes-deSoule Pottery), Weaverville, NC. Pages 51, 112, and 116

Neville French, Buninyong, Victoria, Australia. Page 65

Keiko Fukazawa, Pasadena, CA. Pages 17 and 67

Diana Gillispie (Asheville Tileworks & Pottery), Asheville, NC. Pages 5 and 111

Steven Glass, Richmond, VA. Page 28

John Goodheart, Bloomington, IN. Page 20

Katharine Gotham, Minneapolis, MN. Pages 64 and 65

Carol Gouthro, Seattle, WA. Page 98

Silvie Granatelli (Granatelli Porcelain), Floyd, VA. Pages 18-19, 132, and back cover

Helio Gutierrez (Potters for Peace), Managua, Nicaragua. Page 117

Patricia L. Hankins, Meansville, GA. Page 150

Makoto Hatori, Namegata-Gun, Ibaraki-Ken, Japan. Page 47

Aase Haügaard (Keramiker Aase Haugaard), Risskov, Denmark. Page 44

Audry Yoder Heatwole, Raleigh, NC. Page 125

Ronalee Herrmann (Herrmann-Stolken Porcelain), Santa Barbara, CA. Page 73

Mark Hewitt (W.M. Hewitt Pottery), Pittsboro, NC. Pages 99 and 122

Chris Hill, Wingate, NC. Page 96

Steven Hill (Steven Hill Pottery), Kansas City, MO. Page 78

Sadashi Inuzuka, Ann Arbor, MI. Page 139

Nicholas Joerling (Joerling Pottery), Penland, NC. Pages 48 and 110

Shiho Kanzaki, Shigaraki, Japan. Page 97

Karen Karnes, c/o Garth Clark Gallery, New York, NY. Page 29

Walter Keeler, c/o Garth Clark Gallery, New York, NY. Page 111

Shane M. Keena, Los Angeles, CA. Page 91

Michael J. Knox II, La Crosse, WI. Page 46

Karen Koblitz, Los Angeles, CA. Page 116

Geert Lap, c/o Garth Clark Gallery, New York, NY. Page 98

Dick Lehman, Goshen, IN. Page 55

Leah Leitson, Asheville, NC. Pages 51, 126, and 131

Lola J. Logsdon, Fort Collins, CO. Page 56

Matthew Lyon (Matthew Lyon Studio), Portland, OR. Page 72

Warren MacKenzie, Stillwater, MN. Pages 47 and 109

Peg Malloy, Carbondale, CO. Pages 45 and 67

Lisa Mandelkern, Las Cruces, NM. Page 140

Barbara Mann (Mann Made Designs), Chester, VA. Page 20

Ginny Marsh, Louisville, KY, Page 151

John Martin (Cedar Creek Pottery), Creedmoor, NC. Page 125

Don McCance, Tyrone, GA. Page 122

George McCauley, Helena, MT. Page 29

James and Wendy McNally (Harbour Centre Gallery), Providence Bay, Ontario, Canada. Page 138

Mark Messenger, El Sobrante, CA. Page 46

Ron Meyers, Athens, GA. Pages 18 and 80

Lori Mills, Brockport, NY. Page 153

Coll Minogue, Abercairny, Perthshire, Scotland. Page 122

Shigeru Miyamoto (Ceramic Arts), Honolulu, HI. Page 140

Robert Moore, Logan, UT. Page 125

Judith E. Motzkin (Judy Motzkin Studio), Cambridge, MA. Page 48

Kevin A. Myers, Glendale, CA. Page 47

Hiroshi Nakayama, Worthington, MA. Page 139

Shannon Nelson, Gainesville, FL. Page 65

Laura Nuchols, Spokane, WA. Page 152

Sid Oakley (Cedar Creek Pottery), Creedmoor, NC. Pages 73 and 125

George E. Ohr, c/o Garth Clark Gallery, New York, NY. Page 55

Julie Olson (White Oak Artworks), Cary, NC. Page 125

Jose Ortiz (Potters for Peace), Managua, Nicaragua. Page 116

Ben Owen (1905-1983). Page 138

Ben Owen III (Ben Owen Pottery), Seagrove, NC. Pages 5, 30, and 117

Kreg Richard Owens (Trinity Clay Productions), Alexandria, VA. Page 131

Vernon Owens (Jugtown Pottery), Seagrove, NC. Page 90

M. Oya, Kyoto, Japan. Page 28

Margaret Freeman Patterson, Atlanta, GA. Page 72

Neil Patterson, Philadelphia, PA. Pages 49 and 81

David Pinto, Montego Bay, Jamaica. Page 29

Ted Randall (1914-1985). Page 45

David Regan, c/o Garth Clark Gallery, New York, NY. Page 124

Don Reitz, Clarkdale, AZ. Page 19

Douglass Rankin (Rock Creek Pottery), Bakersville, NC. Page 89

Ole Morten Rokvam, Dallas, TX. Pages 44 and 133

Laurie Rolland (Laurie Rolland Pottery), Sechelt, B.C., Canada. Page 133

Peter Rose, Knoxville, TN. Page 73

Harriet E. Ross, Hartsdale, NY. Page 65

Will Ruggles (Rock Creek Pottery), Bakersville, NC. Page 89

Ruri, Sheridan, OR. Page 96

Michael E. Rutkowsky (Pond Branch Pottery), Green Mountain, NC. Page 66

Robert Sanderson, Crieff, Perthshire, Scotland. Page 18

Laura Saville (Laura Saville Pottery), Atlanta, GA. Page 91

Shelley Schreiber, Denver, CO. Page 110

Norm Schulman, Penland, NC. Pages 5, 50, 72, 78, and 134

Daniel Seagle (1805-1867). Page 28

Bonnie Seeman, Plantation, FL. Page 130

Ellen Shankin, Floyd, VA. Page 89

Rhea S. Shea, Portland OR. Page 71

Alfred Stolken (Herrmann-Stolken Porcelain), Santa Barbara, CA. Page 73

Annette Siffin, Ann Arbor, MI. Page 98

Shari Sikora, Havertown, PA. Page 152

Michael Simon, Colbert, GA. Page 151

Chris Simoncelli, Atlanta, GA. Page 64

Paul Soldner (Soldner Pottery Equipment), Aspen, CO. Page 151

Ian Stainton, Bellefonte, PA. Page 97

Chris Staley, c/o Garth Clark Gallery, New York, NY. Pages 57 and 133

W.B. Stephen (1876-1961). Page 131

Kouji Sugie, Tokoname, Japan. Page 48

Charles Tefft, Atlanta, GA. Page 109

Ikuzi Teraki (Romulus Craft), Washington, VT. Page 19

Beth Thomas, Galveston, TX. Page 91

John Tilton, Alachua, FL. Page 31

Jack Troy, Huntingdon, PA. Page 21

Brad Tucker (Brad Tucker Pottery), Creedmoor, NC. Pages 73 and 90

Tim Turner, Banner Elk, NC. Page 55

Rick Urban (The Mountain Pottery), Dillsboro, NC. Pages 5 and 56

Mike Vatalaro, Pendleton, SC. Page 81

Sandy Vitarelli (Sandy Vitarelli Functional Potter), Maui, HI. Page 123

Peter Voulkos, c/o Perimeter Gallery, Chicago, IL. Pages 45 and 79

Denise Woodward-Detrich, Walhalla, SC. Page 73

Cynthia L. Young, Gibsonia, PA. Page 153

Colleen Zufelt (Zufelt Designs), Wilmington, DE. Page 152

Artists may be contacted directly or through Lark Books (*Wheel-Thrown Ceramics*), 50 College Street, Asheville, NC 28801.

Index